# THE
# PREHISTORIC EARTH

# TIME OF
# THE GIANTS

## THE MIDDLE &
## LATE JURASSIC EPOCHS

# THE PREHISTORIC EARTH

Early Life:
The Cambrian Period

The First Vertebrates:
Oceans of the Paleozoic Era

March Onto Land:
The Silurian Period to the Middle Triassic Epoch

Dawn of the Dinosaur Age:
The Late Triassic & Early Jurassic Epochs

Time of the Giants:
The Middle & Late Jurassic Epochs

Last of the Dinosaurs:
The Cretaceous Period

The Rise of Mammals:
The Paleocene & Eocene Epochs

The Age of Mammals:
The Oligocene & Miocene Epochs

Primates and Human Ancestors:
The Pliocene Epoch

Early Humans:
The Pleistocene & Holocene Epochs

# THE PREHISTORIC EARTH

# TIME OF THE GIANTS

## The Middle & Late Jurassic Epochs

### Thom Holmes

**CHELSEA HOUSE** PUBLISHERS

An imprint of Infobase Publishing

Chelsea House
An imprint of Infobase Publishing
132 West 31st Street
New York NY 10001

**Library of Congress Cataloging-in-Publication Data**

Holmes, Thom.
  Time of the giants / Thom Holmes.
    p. cm. — (The prehistoric Earth)
  Includes bibliographical references and index.
  ISBN 978-0-8160-5961-4 (hardcover)
  1. Dinosaurs—Study and teaching—United States  2. Fossils—Study and teaching—United States.
3. Geology, Stratigraphic—Jurassic. I. Title. II. Series.

  QE861.4.H655 2008
  567.9—dc22            2007045332

Chelsea House books are available at special discounts when purchased in bulk quantities for businesses, associations, institutions, or sales promotions. Please call our Special Sales Department in New York at (212) 967-8800 or (800) 322-8755.

You can find Chelsea House on the World Wide Web at http://www.chelseahouse.com

Text design by Kerry Casey
Cover design by Salvatore Luongo
Section opener images © John Sibbick

Printed in the United States of America

Bang NMSG 10 9 8 7 6 5 4 3 2 1

This book is printed on acid-free paper.

All links and Web addresses were checked and verified to be correct at the time of publication. Because of the dynamic nature of the Web, some addresses and links may have changed since publication and may no longer be valid.

# CONTENTS

# PREFACE

To be curious about the future, one must know something about the past.

Humans have been recording events in the world around them for about 5,300 years. That is how long it has been since the Sumerian people, in a land that is today part of southern Iraq, invented the first known written language. Writing allowed people to document what they saw happening around them. The written word gave a new permanency to life. Language, and writing in particular, made history possible.

History is a marvelous human invention, but how do people know about things that happened before language existed? Or before humans existed? Events that took place before human record keeping began are called *prehistory*. Prehistoric life is, by its definition, any life that existed before human beings existed and were able to record for posterity what was happening in the world around them.

Prehistory is as much a product of the human mind as history. Scientists who specialize in unraveling clues of prehistoric life are called *paleontologists*. They study life that existed before human history, often hundreds of thousands and millions, and even billions, of years in the past. Their primary clues come from **fossils** of animals, plants, and other organisms, as well as geologic evidence about the Earth's **topography** and **climate**. Through the skilled and often clever interpretation of fossils, paleontologists are able to reconstruct the appearances, lifestyles, environments, and relationships of ancient life-forms. While paleontology is grounded in a study of prehistoric life, it draws on many other sciences to complete an accurate picture of the past. Information from the fields of biology, zoology, geology, chemistry, meteorology, and even astrophysics is

6

called into play to help the paleontologist view the past through the lens of today's knowledge.

If a writer were to write a history of all sports, would it be enough to write only about table tennis? Certainly not. On the shelves of bookstores and libraries, however, we find just such a slanted perspective toward the story of the dinosaurs. Dinosaurs have captured our imagination at the expense of many other equally fascinating, terrifying, and unusual creatures. Dinosaurs were not alone in the pantheon of prehistoric life, but it is rare to find a book that also mentions the many other kinds of life that came before and after the dinosaurs.

*The Prehistoric Earth* is a series that explores the evolution of life from its earliest forms 3.5 billion years ago until the emergence of modern humans some 300,000 years ago. Four volumes in the series trace the story of the dinosaurs. Six other volumes are devoted to the kinds of animals that evolved before, during, and after the reign of the dinosaurs. *The Prehistoric Earth* covers the early explosion of life in the oceans; the invasion of the land by the first land animals; the rise of fishes, amphibians, reptiles, mammals, and birds; and the emergence of modern humans.

*The Prehistoric Earth* series is written for readers in middle school and high school. Based on the latest scientific findings in paleontology, *The Prehistoric Earth* is the most comprehensive and up-to-date series of its kind for this age group.

The first volume in the series, *Early Life,* offers foundational information about geologic time, Earth science, fossils, the classification of organisms, and evolution. This volume also begins the chronological exploration of fossil life that explodes with the incredible life-forms of Precambrian time and the Cambrian Period, more than 500 million years ago.

The remaining nine volumes in the series can be read chronologically. Each volume covers a specific geologic time period and describes the major forms of life that lived at that time. The books also trace the geologic forces and climate changes that affected the evolution of life through the ages. Readers of *The Prehistoric Earth* will see the whole picture of prehistoric life take shape. They will learn about forces that affect life on Earth, the directions that life can sometimes take, and ways in which all life-forms depend on each other in the environment. Along the way, readers also will meet many of the scientists who have made remarkable discoveries about the prehistoric Earth.

The language of science is used throughout this series, with ample definition and with an extensive glossary provided in each volume. Important concepts involving geology, evolution, and the lives of early animals are presented logically, step by step. Illustrations, photographs, tables, and maps reinforce and enhance the books' presentation of the story of prehistoric life.

While telling the story of prehistoric life, the author hopes that many readers will be sufficiently intrigued to continue studies on their own. For this purpose, throughout each volume, special "Think About It" sidebars offer additional insights or interesting exercises for readers who wish to explore certain topics. Each book in the series also provides a chapter-by-chapter bibliography of books, journals, and Web sites.

Only about one-tenth of 1 percent of all species of prehistoric animals are known from fossils. A multitude of discoveries remain to be made in the field of paleontology. It is with earnest, best wishes that I hope that some of these discoveries will be made by readers inspired by this series.

—Thom Holmes
Jersey City, New Jersey

# Acknowledgments

I would like to thank the many dedicated and hardworking people at Chelsea House. A special debt of gratitude goes to my editors, Shirley White, Brian Belval, and Frank Darmstadt, for their support and guidance in conceiving and making *The Prehistoric Earth* a reality. Frank and Brian were instrumental in fine-tuning the features of the series as well as accepting my ambitious plan for creating a comprehensive reference for students. Brian greatly influenced the development of the color-illustration program and supported my efforts to integrate the work of some of the best artists in the field, most notably John Sibbick, whose work appears throughout the set. Shirley's excellent questions about the science behind the books contributed greatly to the readability of the result. The excellent copyediting of Mary Ellen Kelly was both thoughtful and vital to shaping the final manuscript. I thank Mary Ellen for her patience as well as her valuable review and suggestions that help make the books a success.

I am privileged to have worked with some of the brightest minds in paleontology on this series. Jerry D. Harris, the director of paleontology at Dixie State College in St. George, Utah, reviewed the draft of *Dawn of the Dinosaur Age* and made many important suggestions that affected the course of the work. Jerry also wrote the Foreword for the volume.

In many ways, a set of books such as this requires years of preparation. Some of the work is educational, and I owe much gratitude to Dr. Peter Dodson of the University of Pennsylvania for his gracious and inspiring tutelage over the years. Another dimension of preparation requires experience digging fossils, and for giving me these opportunities I thank my friends and colleagues who have taken me into the field with them, including Phil Currie, Rodolfo Coria,

Matthew Lammana, and Ruben Martinez. Finally comes the work needed to put thoughts down on paper and complete the draft of a book, a process that always takes many more hours than I plan on. I thank Anne for bearing with my constant state of busy-ness and for helping me remember the important things in life. You are an inspiration to me. I also thank my daughter, Shaina, the genius in the family and another inspiration, for always being supportive and humoring her father's obsession with prehistoric life.

# FOREWORD

Learning about organisms alive today—be they animals, plants, fungi, single-celled creatures, or bacteria—is relatively easy. We have zoos, botanical gardens, preserves, and laboratories in which various organisms can be observed while they are alive. There are also endless shelves of books devoted to virtually any kind of organism, and one can read those books if one cannot make it to where the organisms live.

Learning about extinct organisms is much more difficult. As it is impossible to actually watch an extinct organism do what it would do on a day-to-day basis, we naturally know less about extinct organisms than we do about most extant things. To learn about extinct organisms, we have to turn to rocks—to the fossil record, the only record we have of life that was around before we had zoos, botanical gardens, preserves, and labs. It is from this past life that everything alive today came, and our understanding of any kind of organism is incomplete unless we also understand that organism's evolutionary history. Moreover, it would be impossible to predict what life in the future might be like without an understanding of how life in the past changed and evolved. This is why paleontology—the study of fossil organisms of all kinds—is so important.

Over the past few hundred years, paleontologists have amassed so much knowledge about the life of the past that it has become difficult to learn about all of it. This series of books, *The Prehistoric Earth*, is designed to give readers a sort of guided tour of ancient life, from its very beginnings to the modern world. Note that this series is not just about dinosaurs, which constitute only a very tiny fraction of all things that have ever lived; virtually all forms of life are covered to varying degrees in *The Prehistoric Earth*. Coverage such as this is a daunting task, but it is one that Thom Holmes has tackled successfully; in this series, he literally provides something for everyone. If this book, the fifth volume in the series, is offering you your first look, I highly recommend getting and reading the previous volumes to help put the information contained in this book into the best possible context.

The Late Triassic origin of dinosaurs and the Early Jurassic beginning of their rise to dominate the Mesozoic world are the topic of the book *Dawn of the Dinosaur Age*. This book, *Time of the Giants*, picks up the story in the Middle Jurassic, when dinosaurs really begin to become the dominant land animals that make their kind famous. Some dinosaurs attained truly astounding sizes, but many (perhaps most) remained relatively small. In many ways, it is the small dinosaurs that are most relevant to humans today, but it is the giants that are so unlike any living thing that they demand attention and create awe and wonder.

Some of the animals about which you'll read in *Time of the Giants* probably will already be familiar to you. Others will be very new, either because they have been discovered only recently or, more likely, because their stories do not often get told outside of the technical literature. Even if these animals are familiar, however, prepare to have some of your preconceptions of them shattered. New research on these "old" animals has revealed that many ideas about them, formulated a hundred or more years ago, are wrong. That, of course, is how science works: by investigating old hypotheses with the aid of new data to see whether the old ideas hold up or whether a different explanation is in order. Tossing out old and outdated information in exchange for newer, better-supported material is never a bad thing!

Thom Holmes does a terrific job of pulling together a wide variety of what may seem to be disparate bits of information to tell the stories of all kinds of dinosaurs, and by doing so demonstrates that what we now know about dinosaurs is actually pretty astonishing. As a result, this book is not only up to date but also a highly accurate portrait of what we currently known about Middle and Late Jurassic dinosaur life. A beautiful and exciting ancient world is made more amazing by the vivid depictions Holmes provides of that world's denizens as they lived. You will not be disappointed.

—Dr. Jerry D. Harris
Director of Paleontology
Dixie State College
St. George, Utah

# INTRODUCTION

The story of the **evolution** of **dinosaurs**, which began in the late Triassic and Early Jurassic Epochs, continued in the Middle and Late Jurassic Epochs and is told in *Time of the Giants*. Herein is the story of an astounding and geologically stable period in the Earth's history, during which dinosaurs seemed to grow to unfettered sizes and succeeded in spreading their domination to all parts of the planet.

*Time of the Giants* investigates those dinosaurs that arose during the Middle and Late Jurassic Epochs, a span of 30 million years that lasted from about 175 million to 145 million years ago. This was the time of the largest land animals ever to walk the Earth—the sauropods. These giants were not alone, however; other kinds of dinosaurs were diversifying rapidly as well. Most notably, predatory dinosaurs began their own trend towards **gigantism**, and plated and armored **herbivores** developed prolifically, filling ecological spaces not tread upon by the long-necked giants.

Another book in this series, *Dawn of the Dinosaur Age,* defines and introduces the dinosaurs, tracing their origins and their early evolution. After exploring the classification of dinosaurs into two major groups—the **Saurischia**, or "lizard-hipped" dinosaurs, and the **Ornithischia**, or "bird-hipped" dinosaurs—*Dawn of the Dinosaur Age* discusses the traits and lifestyles of the early dinosaurs, especially the theropods and sauropodomorphs.

This book, *Time of the Giants*, expands on those two lines of dinosaurs by introducing the members of each group that were part of the great Jurassic radiation of dinosaurs. The ornithischians— barely known at all from the Late Triassic and Early Jurassic—play a more significant role as the Jurassic **Period** continues and are represented by increasingly diverse groups of highly specialized plant eaters.

## OVERVIEW OF *TIME OF THE GIANTS*

*Time of the Giants* begins by looking at the geological and ecological conditions that created opportunities for the expansion of dinosaurs in the Middle and Late Jurassic Epochs. Chapter 1 describes widespread changes to ocean and land environments, including worldwide climate changes that served as catalysts for the spread of dinosaurs. One factor that deserves a close look is the way the evolution of plants interacted with the evolution of dinosaurs to create a variety of ecological niches for dinosaurian herbivores.

Chapter 2 explores the broad range of the largest of all land animals, the sauropods. Discussions of sauropod anatomical traits, feeding habits, nesting practices, locomotion, and **metabolism** bring together many lines of scientific evidence to portray these giants as living, breathing creatures. This chapter also tells the story of the first sauropod discoveries and describes the changing scientific images of sauropods over the past 150 years.

Chapter 3 concentrates on the theropods, or carnivorous dinosaurs. It continues the story of predatory dinosaurs by examining widely diverse theropods of all sizes that first appeared during the latter Jurassic Period. Among these were the first evolutionary experiments in gigantic carnivores, including *Allosaurus.* The chapter explores the attack and feeding styles of predatory dinosaurs and tackles the subject of dinosaur intelligence. The chapter introduces major families of theropods, including the coelurosaurs; among the coelurosaurs were some small **predators** that led to the evolution of birds. The first bird, *Archaeopteryx,* is also a part of the story of Jurassic theropods. In Chapter 3, its significance in the study of bird origins is explored.

Chapter 4 introduces the first well-known ornithischian dinosaurs, the armored and plated herbivores. Among them are Stegosauria and Ankylosauria. The origins, traits, diversity, and lifestyles of these animals are detailed, along with a review of the kinds of plants that enabled them to define an ecological niche for themselves in the world of giant herbivores.

Each chapter uses an abundance of tables, maps, figures, and photos to depict the conditions, habitats, and changing evolutionary patterns that affected the lives of the early dinosaurs and their kin. Several chapters also include "Think About It" sidebars that focus on interesting issues, people, history, and discoveries related to Mesozoic life.

*Time of the Giants* builds on the same foundational principles of geology, fossils, and the study of life that are introduced in other volumes of *The Prehistoric Earth*. Readers who want to refresh their knowledge of certain basic terms and principles in the study of past life may wish to consult the glossary that begins on page 131 of *Time of the Giants*. Perhaps most important to keep in mind are the basic rules governing evolution: that the process of evolution is set in motion first by the traits inherited by individuals and then by the interaction of a **population** of a species with those traits with its habitat. Changes that enable the population to survive accumulate generation after generation, often producing and allowing species to adapt to changing conditions in the world around them. As Charles Darwin (1809–1882) explained, "The small differences distinguishing varieties of the same species steadily tend to increase, till they equal the greater differences between species of the same genus, or even of distinct genera." These are the rules of nature that served to stoke the engine of evolution during the Paleozoic and that gave rise to forms of life whose descendants still populate the Earth.

# SECTION ONE:
## THE WORLD OF
## THE DINOSAURS

# 1

# The Middle and Late Jurassic Epochs

To understand the past requires imagination as much as it requires facts. One place where people learn about the past is school. The history of human civilization can be laid out on a timeline to show the events that shaped the development of humankind. An understanding of the peoples and cultures of the past requires imagination, but such an understanding is readily attainable because the people of the past were driven by much the same motivations—whether emotional, political, or survival—that drive the people of the present. The civilized people of the past were much like the people of today. The layout of the continents, the climate, and the topography of the Earth have varied little, except for human-drawn political borders, during the development of civilization. A person transported back in time 2,000 or 3,000 years would find a planet that, geographically at least, resembled the Earth of today in most ways.

To understand life before humans, especially the deep past of many millions of years ago, presents more of a challenge. During the days of the dinosaurs, the Earth was not the same as the Earth of today. A person flung back in time some 150 million years would not recognize the shapes of the continents or the plants, animals, and climate zones that held sway during that time. It was very much a foreign world compared to that which we know today.

**Paleontologists** grapple with geologic and fossil evidence to paint a picture of the world of the dinosaurs. The accuracy of this picture depends on the availability of geologic and fossil strata from spans of the Mesozoic Era. This chapter examines evidence

19

## EVOLUTIONARY MILESTONES OF THE MESOZOIC ERA

| Period | Epoch | Span (millions of years ago) | Duration (millions of years) | Organismal Milestones |
|---|---|---|---|---|
| Triassic | Early Triassic | 251–245 | 6 | Diversification and distribution of amniotes, particularly synapsid and diapsid reptiles |
| | Middle Triassic | 245–228 | 17 | Euryapsid marine reptiles |
| | Late Triassic | 228–200 | 28 | Early turtles, dinosaurs, crocodylomorphs, pterosaurs, and mammals |
| | Mass extinction | | | Casualties: dicynodonts, carnivorous cynodonts, phytosaurs, placodonts, nothosaurs |
| Jurassic | Early Jurassic | 200–175 | 25 | Radiation of carnivorous and herbivorous dinosaurs, first crocodyliforms |
| | Middle Jurassic | 175–161 | 14 | Rise of armored and plated dinosaurs, rise of sauropods |
| | Late Jurassic | 161–145 | 16 | Diversification of sauropods, theropods, the first birds |
| Cretaceous | Early Cretaceous | 145–100 | 45 | Continued diversification of dinosaurs, birds, marine reptiles, and pterosaurs |
| | Late Cretaceous | 100–65.5 | 35 | Rise of large theropods, horned dinosaurs, hadrosaurs |
| | Mass extinction | | | Casualties: Dinosaurs, marine reptiles, pterosaurs |

for the geologic and climatic conditions that influenced the evolution of the **flora** and **fauna** of the Middle and Late Jurassic Epochs.

## SHAPING THE WORLD OF THE DINOSAURS

The Mesozoic **Era** stretched from 65.5 million to 251 million years ago and thus had a total span of 186 million years. The Mesozoic is divided into three periods of time, beginning with the Triassic Period, moving to the middle or Jurassic Period, and concluding with the Cretaceous. Each of these periods is subdivided into smaller units (early, middle and late, except the Cretaceous which does not have an official "middle"), called epochs. The Early and Middle Triassic Epochs witnessed dramatic changes to the ecology of the Earth and the **extinction** of older forms of vertebrates carried over from the Paleozoic Era. Among them were several prominent lines of **carnivorous** and herbivorous reptiles. From those reptilian roots rose the first dinosaurs in the Late Triassic, about 228 millions years ago. Dinosaurs became the story of the Mesozoic, dominating life for 162.5 million years until the dramatic extinction of the last of their kind 65.5 million years ago.

The Late Triassic and Early Jurassic Epochs, a span of 53 million years, were a time of evolutionary innovation for dinosaurs. It was during that time that the two fundamental lineages of dinosaurs—the Saurischia and the Ornithischia—first took shape. In those earliest of dinosaurs can be seen clues to the great clades of dinosaur descendants to follow. Small theropods such as *Eoraptor* (Late Triassic, Argentina) and *Coelophysis* (Late Triassic, New Mexico) set the mold for the body plan of all theropods to follow. The early sauropod *Vulcanodon* (Early Jurassic, Zimbabwe), with its long neck and tail, small head, bulky body, and four-legged posture, presaged the giant, long-necked herbivores to follow. Even though the first ornithischians are very poorly known, examples such as *Lesothosaurus* (Early Jurassic, Lesotho) provide a preview of the sophisticated plant-eating jaws and teeth that became the hallmark of most of the ornithischians that followed. The evolution of these earliest dinosaurs took place at the dawn of the dinosaur age, at a time before the span covered in this book.

The next important stage of dinosaur evolution occurred during the Middle and Late Jurassic Epochs, the span that is the subject of *Time of the Giants*. The Jurassic Period marks the middle span of the Age of Dinosaurs.

Many gaps exist in the fossil record of dinosaurs. For example, little is known from the Middle and Late Jurassic of eastern North America. Fossils of Late Jurassic age are also scarce in South

America and Australia. What was happening to dinosaurs, plants, and other organisms from those time periods and places is a matter of speculation; paleontologists do their best to make educated guesses about the geologic and climatic conditions of those areas based on knowledge from other parts of the world.

Dinosaurs of the Middle Jurassic are poorly known except for two regions of the world, Europe—most significantly, England and Scotland and, to a lesser degree, France, Germany, and eastern Russia—and China, especially the province of Sichuan. Remains of Middle Jurassic dinosaurs from North America consist primarily of fossil footprints. Evidence of dinosaurs from this time period in the Southern Hemisphere (South America, Africa, Antarctica, and Australia) is very scrappy. The total of undisputed fossil sites for Middle Jurassic dinosaurs numbers only 69, 20 percent of which lack skeletal material and include only trace fossils such as footprints.

Dinosaurs of the Late Jurassic are much better known. They are found to some extent on all continents except Australia and Antarctica, and fossil riches from the Late Jurassic are found in abundance in North America, Europe, Asia, South America, and Africa. Unlike most Middle Jurassic fossil sites, with their spotty remains, some of the best known localities for Late Jurassic dinosaurs have yielded whole and partial skeletons of more than 35 individual **species** of dinosaurs, both large and small. Such tremendous stores of fossils and associated evidence for plants and climate conditions have allowed paleontologists to reconstruct a vivid picture of life during the Middle and Late Jurassic.

From the standpoint of continental shifts, the Mesozoic Era was notable for slow but dramatic changes to the sizes and shapes of the world's terrestrial and oceanic bodies. The Mesozoic was not without its geologic catastrophes; for the most part, however, the shifts in climates and landmasses and associated changes in the herbivorous food supply took place at a rate with which vertebrate evolution could keep pace. Dinosaurs and their **archosaurian** kin ruled for nearly 163 million years, until the end of the Cretaceous Period, when a combination of massive volcanic activity in Asia, climate changes, and asteroid hits shook the Earth and sent these creatures into oblivion.

The dominant geologic event of the Mesozoic was the breakup of the supercontinent **Pangaea**. All of the currently known continents were joined as one enormous landmass at the beginning of the Mesozoic Era. By the end of the Mesozoic, however, the terrestrial bodies of the world had separated into forms that approximate those seen today. Pangaea began to split apart in the Early Jurassic, first dividing into two landmasses. The northern landmass, which geologists call **Laurasia**, included areas that became North America, Europe, and Asia. The southern landmass, known as **Gondwana**, included the regions that would eventually become today's South America, Africa, India, Australia, and Antarctica.

Before dividing up, Pangaea was bounded on the west by the **Panthalassic Ocean** and on the east by the **Tethys Ocean**. The Atlantic Ocean began to appear in the middle of Pangaea as tectonic plates separated and continental landmasses radiated outward, moving to the north and south from the equator. Water displaced by the rise of massive mid-ocean ridges was pushed onto the lower elevations of terrestrial habitats. Continental areas that today are associated with North and South America, Europe, central Asia, and northern Africa were the sites of extensive inland seas. During the Cretaceous Period, North America had a shallow inland sea that stretched down the middle of the landmass from what is now Alaska to the Gulf of Mexico.

Geologically, the Jurassic was perhaps the quietest period during the Mesozoic. It was a time of limited mountain building and volcanic activity. Instead, there is much evidence worldwide that the Jurassic was a time during which many great highlands became eroded, thereby creating large areas of low-lying land. Despite the low profile of most continental interiors, during the Jurassic the surrounding oceans did not encroach on the land, with the

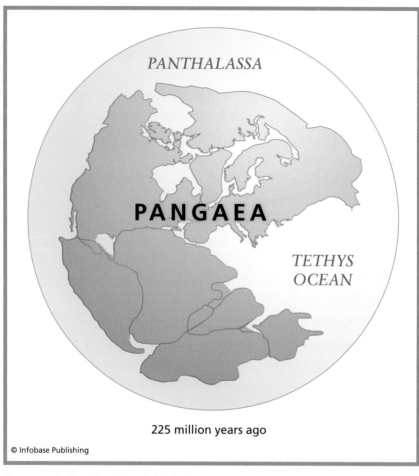

225 million years ago

© Infobase Publishing

**Pangaea during the Triassic Period**

exception of some continental margins. This stable period in the history of the continents encouraged the formation of freshwater lakes, rivers, and floodplains. One extraordinarily large freshwater lake formed in Australia. The lake covered nearly 300,000 square miles (777,000 square kilometers)—about the size of the state of Texas. Sediments left behind by that lake are an astounding 7,000 feet (2,134 meters) thick. Some parts of western North America were also subject to massive land deposits, especially on what is today the

Colorado Plateau, where some sedimentary deposits of sandstone reach thicknesses of hundreds of feet.

Further evidence in North America for erosional deposits is the widespread Morrison Formation along the western interior. The formation is an extensive area of alluvial deposits covering 750,000 square miles (1,942,000 square kilometers). Known as an abundant source of Late Jurassic dinosaur fossils, the Morrison Formation was a broad, sandy, fan-shaped, or alluvial, lowland formed at the juncture of smaller streams with ravines and larger streams.

Most of central Asia and Asia were above sea level during the Jurassic; the same is assumed for Africa, although only a few Jurassic-age deposits are found there. The gap now formed by the Atlantic Ocean between North America and Europe was much narrower during the Jurassic Period. The similarity of some fossils from the Gulf of Mexico region and Europe suggests that a temporary, sediment based land bridge may have once spanned the Atlantic gap as late as the Late Jurassic and Early Cretaceous. Likewise, Africa and South America were still linked by a solid land bridge through the Jurassic Period and into the earliest Cretaceous. Proof of this comes in part from the similarity of dinosaur and other taxa found on both continents in rocks dating from those times.

## CLIMATES AND HABITATS

The Middle and Late Jurassic Epochs were evenly warm and temperate across the globe; there is no evidence of polar ice caps at that time. Widespread warmth enveloped the Earth and allowed dinosaurs to roam to every habitable corner of the planet. Today, widespread coal deposits and fossil evidence of marine coral and reefs located 2,000 miles (3,218 kilometers) north of where they exist today all provide supporting evidence that the Jurassic world was warm. In lands to the north that now are extremely cold, such as Greenland and parts of northern Europe, there grew such mild-climate plants as ginkgo trees and certain conifers. None of these plants could have survived subfreezing temperatures on a regular basis.

The evidence for great sandy deposits in Australia and North America suggests that some parts of the planet were drier and more arid than others. Coal deposits, on the other hand, indicate a more humid habitat; such deposits are found in places as widespread as British Columbia and Vancouver Island—both in western Canada—and in Mexico.

An innovative study published in 2000 by paleontologists Peter McA. Rees, Alfred M. Ziegler, and Paul J. Valdes used the morphology (shape) of Late Jurassic fossil leaves to create a map of likely worldwide climate zones. Leaves are particularly excellent gauges of climate because they represent a direct means by which plants interact with the environment. The shape and biology of a leaf is adapted by evolution to optimize prevailing climatic conditions. Jurassic plants were particularly diverse and were distributed in zones across terrestrial ecosystems. The research team found that mid-latitude plants were the most diverse; flora in those latitudes included forests mixed with ferns, cycads, horsetails, seed ferns, and conifers. Patchy forests of small-leafed cycads and conifers were present at lower latitudes. Polar vegetation consisted mainly of large-leafed conifers and ginkgo trees. Based on their analysis of the climate-related characteristics of such plants, the team was able to identify several predominant climate zones across the planet. These included zones of tropical, desert, and warm temperate conditions over much of Earth's land area.

Analysis of the oxygen isotope content of Mesozoic marine fossils provides additional support for a temperate world climate. Samples taken from locations in North America, Europe, and Russia show that the temperature of shallow marine environments ranged from between 60°F and 75°F (15°C and 24°C), making for a relatively warm day at or near the beach most of the time.

A key reason for the moderating of global temperature during the Jurassic Period was the breakup of Pangaea. The division of the

Jurassic landscape

giant landmass into smaller continents made all land more suscep-
tible to temperature changes moderated by ocean currents. During
the Mesozoic, the lack of ice caps meant that the Earth was covered
by more water than during the latter stages of the Paleozoic. Because
water is a tremendous sponge for solar radiation, the oceans became
warm; ocean currents that now could flow around the equator,
where the most intense and directly sunlight is received, collected
and distributed heat to the north and south, providing a more
evenly temperate world climate.

*(continues on page 31)*

# THINK ABOUT IT

## Mesozoic Plants and the Evolution of Dinosaur Herbivory

When two species of organisms influence each other's evolution, **coevolution** is taking place. Coevolution is a change, through natural selection, in the genetic makeup of one species in response to a genetic change in another. Some well-documented examples occur between birds and plants. In the lowland forests of Central and South America, for example, hermit hummingbirds have evolved a long, curved beak especially suited for feeding from the curved flowers of the *Heliconia* plant. Another example comes from the Galapagos Islands—the famous setting for many of Charles Darwin's formative observations about natural selection. Different species of Galapagos finches have adapted beak sizes suited for eating seeds of particular sizes.

There appears to be a coevolutionary relationship between herbivorous dinosaurs and the development of Mesozoic plants. It was probably not a coincidence that the first large, long-necked herbivorous dinosaurs—the "prosauropods"—appeared alongside conifer trees that were growing taller and taller. What is not fully understood is whether the conifers were growing taller to get out of reach of low-browsing "prosauropods" or whether "prosauropods" were standing upright to reach taller plants that were out of reach of shorter browsing or grazing animals. In either case, a symbiotic relationship between the height of plants and the size of dinosaurs appeared to have begun by the Late Triassic.

Several researchers have linked the jaw mechanisms and sizes of herbivorous dinosaurs with the kinds of plants that were prevalent in their habitats. Paleontologists David Fastovsky, Joshua B. Smith, and others have made a convincing case for associating various kinds of plant-eating dinosaurs with tiering—different levels at which herbivorous dinosaurs ate according to their height and the size of plants in the habitat. The accompanying table summarizes this tiering phenomenon for different groups of herbivores.

### COEVOLUTION OF HERBIVOROUS DINOSAURS AND MESOZOIC PLANTS

| Dinosaur Taxon | Plant-Eating Adaptation | Tier | Likely Diet |
|---|---|---|---|
| "Prosauropods" | Plucking teeth; gut processing with gastroliths | High browsing (3 to 10 feet; 1 to 3 m) | Conifers (evergreens); cycads; ginkgo trees |
| Sauropods— Diplodocids | Cropping teeth | Low to intermediate browsing (3 to 24 feet; 1 to 7 m) and some grazing (less than 3 feet; less than 1 m) | Conifers (evergreens); cycads; ginkgos |
| Sauropods— Camarasaurids, Brachiosaurids, Titanosaurs, others | Cropping teeth | Medium to very high browsing (3 to 33 feet; 1 to 10 m) | Conifers (evergreens); ginkgo trees |
| Ankylosaurs | Cropping beak; puncture chewing | Low browsing (3 feet; 1 m) | Seed ferns; ferns; club mosses; cycads; horsetails |
| Stegosaurs | Cropping beak; puncture chewing | Low browsing (3 feet; 1 m) | Seed ferns; ferns; club mosses; cycads; horsetails |
| Heterodonto-saurids | Cropping beak; puncture chewing; gut processing with gastroliths | Low browsing (3 feet; 1 m) | Seed ferns; ferns; club mosses; cycads; horsetails |
| Iguanodontids | Cropping beak; shearing and low-grade chewing | Low to intermediate browsing (3 to 10 feet; 1 to 3 m) | Seed ferns; ferns; club mosses; cycads; horsetails; conifers (evergreens); ginkgo trees |

*(continues)*

*(continued)*

| Dinosaur Taxon | Plant-Eating Adaptation | Tier | Likely Diet |
|---|---|---|---|
| Hadrosaurids | Cropping beak; shearing and high-grade grinding with teeth | Low to intermediate browsing (3 to 13 feet; 1 to 4 m) | Seed ferns; ferns; club mosses; cycads; horsetails; conifers (evergreens); ginkgo trees; flowering plants |
| Ceratopsids | Cropping beak; high-grade slicing and grinding with teeth | Low to intermediate browsing (3 to 7 feet; 1 to 2 m) | Seed ferns; ferns; club mosses; cycads; horsetails; flowering plants |

Data based on Fastovsky and Smith, 2004, from *The Dinosauria.*

The crowning achievement of sophisticated plant-eating jaw morphology developed late in the history of dinosaurs. The ornithischians of the Late Cretaceous—particularly the later horned dinosaurs and hadrosaurids—had dental batteries so well suited for chewing plants that they rival those seen in later mammals. This burst of innovation in the chewing mechanisms of later dinosaurs occurred at the same time as the rise of angiosperms—the flowering plants. Angiosperms are more nutritious than gymnosperms and reproduce and grow more quickly; therefore, they can recover better from having parts removed. Because of this, some researchers maintain that the Late Cretaceous burst of ornithischian dinosaur evolution was literally fueled by the flowering plants, a new and better source of nutrition for dinosaurs. There is one conundrum in this scenario, though. Evidence for the gut contents of Late Cretaceous ornithischians shows that they were still eating primarily gymnosperms—conifers, evergreens and the like. Still, the possible coevolutionary relationship between the rise of flowering plants and the last of the great plant-eating dinosaurs is too suggestive to be ignored, so perhaps it is merely a matter of time and better fossil evidence before the picture becomes entirely clear.

*(continued from page 27)*

# BIOGEOGRAPHY AND THE EVOLUTION OF THE DINOSAURS

The evolution of new species is mitigated by a number of factors, including the genetic makeup of an organism and environmental influences on **natural selection**. The place or habitat where an animal lives has much to do with its ability to find a mate, reproduce, and continue the species. Genetics aside, the evolution of new species is often affected by geographic and climatic influences on a species.

The goal of the science of **paleobiogeography** is to explain the distribution of extinct plants and animals. Paleontologist Ralph Molnar has taken a close look at how geography plays an important role in the continuance and evolution of dinosaur species. Molnar believes that paleobiogeography reveals much more than simply which dinosaurs inhabited which landmasses. "It also illuminates," he explains, "dinosaurian evolution and features of tetrapod evolution in general. The existence of dinosaurs in the tropics, near the poles, and in deserts shows that climate was not a limiting factor in dinosaurian distribution and evolution."

The study of Mesozoic geography and continental plate movements brings into play two geologically based concepts related to the distribution of dinosaurs. One theory, called **vicariance biogeography**, depicts distributions taking place by the movement of continents. As the continents moved, so too, did all of the plants and animals riding on their surfaces. The history and movement of organisms, then, are considered as part of the history of continental drift, changes in ocean configurations, and the isolation and recombination of landmasses and the organisms that lived on them. Because continental drift is a slow process, vicariance is also considered to exert a long-term influence on animal distribution. For example, if whole populations of dinosaurs remained on a given landmass, their distributions would eventually, after millions of years, be influenced by the shifting and colliding of continents and all effects that would have on climate and habitat.

Another core concept behind paleobiogeography is that of **dispersalist biogeography**. According to this theory, moving animals, rather than moving continents, are most significant. Given the existence of land bridges—even temporary ones—between continents, animals can move from one geographic location to another much more quickly than the time it takes continents to drift. Such widespread movement, perhaps over several generations of a species, could eventually place its members in a habitat that was significantly different than that of its ancestors. The resulting evolutionary **adaptations** to habitat and climate could result, over time, in a new species.

The current view of paleobiogeography synthesizes vicariance and dispersalist theories, assuming that each plays a role in shaping the course of evolution. In either case, the development of a new species seems to occur most frequently when two or more parts of the same population become separated by some impassable geologic barrier. Mountains, deserts, and bodies of water are examples of geologic barriers. If the barrier persists long enough—for the time it takes for many generations to reproduce—the separate populations may accumulate enough genetic changes to make reproduction between them impossible if ever they meet again: They would be two separate and distinct species. Just how this might happen is not too difficult to imagine.

Land bridges are a means for animals to disperse from one continent to another. The appearance of a land bridge can facilitate the connection of two populations that were previously separated. During Mesozoic time, as Pangaea (and later Laurasia and Gondwana) split apart, the appearance or disappearance of land bridges was a significant factor in the ability of dinosaurs and other animals to disperse across continents.

The disappearance of a land bridge leads to **geographic isolation**, another key influence on the evolution of species. This may occur as continents break apart, as sea levels rise to form islands, or by means of mountain building and other naturally occurring geologic events that separate once-joined populations. The separate parts of a population that have become isolated from each other by the geologic barrier eventually diverge genetically and form news species with unique traits. Island populations provide a dramatic example of geographic isolation. On the grandest of scales, the directions taken by dinosaur evolution in South America, Australia, and Madagascar during the Late Cretaceous—when these landmasses were essentially large islands, unconnected to other landmasses—provide examples of species formation that diverged significantly from their distant ancestors that lived when these same continents were joined.

## SUMMARY

This chapter examined evidence for the geologic and climatic conditions that influenced the evolution of the flora and fauna of the Middle and Late Jurassic Epochs.

1. The middle span of the "Age of Dinosaurs" is represented by the Middle and Late Jurassic epochs, a 30 million-year period during which dinosaurs greatly diversified and often grew to huge sizes.
2. The fossil record of Middle Jurassic dinosaurs is poor, primarily consisting of specimens from Great Britain and China. Dinosaurs of the Late Jurassic are much better known, with excellent fossil specimens having been found on all continents except Australia and Antarctica.
3. Geologically, the Mesozoic Era is noted for the gradual breakup of the supercontinent Pangaea into the pieces that would become today's continents.
4. The climate of the Mesozoic Era was evenly temperate over most of the globe.
5. Paleobiogeography is the study of the geographic distribution of extinct organisms.

**6.** The evolution of new species is influenced by geographic features that affect the distribution of animals. Land bridges can broaden the distribution of a species and lead to new species. So, too, can geographic isolation be caused by impassable geographic barriers such as bodies of water, mountains, and deserts.

# SECTION TWO:
## JURASSIC DINOSAURS

# 2

# THE SAUROPODS: HERBIVOROUS GIANTS

Before the familiar images of *Tyrannosaurus, Triceratops, Stego-saurus*, and other iconic dinosaurs of the American West were widely known, the most familiar image of a dinosaur was that of *Brontosaurus*, a sauropod. It was in 1877, under the guidance of American paleontologist Edward Drinker Cope (1840–1897), that the first scientific *restoration*—or illustration—of a dinosaur skeleton on paper was produced. Cope chose as his subject the large sauropod *Camarasaurus*. He created a life-sized illustration of the skeleton and presented it at a scientific meeting, but it was never published. In 1883, Othniel Charles Marsh (1831–1899) produced the first widely published illustration of a dinosaur skeleton. Marsh made an appealing choice in selecting the spectacularly huge *Bron-tosaurus* (now *Apatosaurus*) as the first of his many discoveries to be drawn scientifically. The image of this long-necked behemoth became the first broadly distributed and accurate drawing of a dinosaur to gain the public's attention. Even the animal's given name had a sensational ring to it: "thunder lizard"—a dinosaur so huge that it shook the ground when it walked by. One might say that *Brontosaurus* was the first rock star of dinosaurs.

Sauropods were the tallest, heaviest, and longest animals ever to walk the Earth; of all animals that ever existed, only whales got bigger, and they, of course, cannot walk on land. Sauropods were members of the saurischian **clade** known as **Sauropodomorpha** ("lizard foot form"). Evolutionary adaptations in body size in a

*(continues on page 40)*

Barosaurus

# THINK ABOUT IT

## The Evolving Images of Sauropod Dinosaurs

The scientific study of sauropod dinosaurs has been replete with its own evolution in the depiction of these most giant of all land animals. *Cetiosaurus* was the first named sauropod, in 1841, but when Sir Richard Owen (1804–1892) first classified it, he had little to go by except five vertebrae, some scattered pieces of limb, and a chunk of rib. He thought it was a giant crocodile, so attempts at illustrating it as a dinosaur did not emerge until much later, when better specimens were available.

The history of illustrating sauropods closely parallels the various debates surrounding their lifestyle. Were sauropods primarily aquatic? Could they lift their heads high and bend their necks with great flexibility? Did they have a robust terrestrial lifestyle, or were they sluggish, sauntering creatures?

The dinosaur bone rush in America during the 1870s uncovered the first remarkably complete specimens of sauropods and inspired the first attempts to create scientifically accurate illustrations of them. As mentioned, Cope was arguably the first paleontologist to reconstruct a dinosaur skeleton on paper, and he did so with great gusto. The life-sized illustration of *Camarasaurus* that he created in 1877 depicted a creature with a sturdy, upright posture and a robust vertebral column that paralleled the ground from head to tail. This view was remarkably modern by today's standards, but only a year later, in 1878, Cope's view of sauropods had begun to change. On a brown paper bag, Cope sketched a scene of living sauropods that spent their time almost fully submerged in the water and fed on bottom-dwelling plants. Almost 20 years later, in 1897, the first great dinosaur artist, Charles Knight (1874–1953), transformed Cope's sketch of submerged sauropods into a drawing that was reproduced in the *Century*, a popular magazine of the day.

In 1883, Othniel Marsh completed his influential drawing of a complete skeleton of *Brontosaurus*, now known as *Apatosaurus*. Like Cope, Marsh thought that sauropods were sluggish swamp dwellers, and his beautiful illustration featured a droopy neck and a dragging tail.

*Apatosaurus*, by Charles R. Knight

Around the start of the twentieth century, the debate over sauropod lifestyles began to heat up. Artists and scientists alike began to wonder whether these creatures were better suited for life on land or in the water. Working with paleontologist Henry Fairfield Osborn (1857–1935) of the American Museum of Natural History, Knight began to hedge his bets in his portrayals of *Apatosaurus*. Rather than depicting sauropods as either aquatic or terrestrial, Knight began to show them as both in the same paintings, one individual firmly entrenched in the water and others standing about on dry land. Knight is, to this day, the most often imitated artist of dinosaurs, and his images that combined aquatic and terrestrial sauropods became the accepted approach to illustrating sauropods for 80 years.

Over time, images of sauropods have undergone some extremely strange transformations. In 1906, believing that sauropods may have had a sprawling posture, model makers Otto Falkenbach (1878–1952) and Charles Falkenbach of the American Museum of Natural History created a scale model of a creeping brontosaur. This image was questioned in 1908 by an American paleontologist, Oliver P. Hay (1846–1930), and a German, Gustav Tornier (1859–1938). Each man took potshots at the Falkenbach

(continues)

*(continued)*

reconstruction. Both argued for an even more extreme sprawling posture that would have required the dinosaurs to drag their bellies. Though this view was renounced by other paleontologists, the view of sauropods as lazy, partly-aquatic creatures remained in vogue for many years. This popular view of water-loving sauropods was reinforced by such world-famous paintings as the one by Rudolf Zallinger (1919–1995) that appeared on the cover of *Life* magazine in 1953.

The evolution of sauropod illustration began to come full circle in 1986, when paleontologist Robert Bakker (b. 1945) published his enthusiastic arguments for fully terrestrial, active sauropods. Bakker's extreme sauropods inspired today's generation of artists. In many ways, however, the current depiction of *Apatosaurus* with a long neck and tail held aloft and parallel to the ground is remarkably similar to Cope's first spectacular illustration in 1877.

*(continued from page 36)*

land animal have never been pushed to the anatomical, physiological, and metabolic extremes that were present in the largest of the sauropodomorphs.

The clade Sauropodomorpha is divided into two groups that had a common ancestor but diverged on two separate lines of large, herbivorous dinosaurs. The earliest group was that of the "Prosauropoda," which lived during the Late Triassic and Early Jurassic Epochs before being supplanted by the second group, the **Sauropoda**. The "prosauropods" are detailed in *Dawn of the Dinosaurs*, a companion volume of *The Prehistoric Earth* series. The sauropods had roots in the Late Triassic but did not begin to radiate widely until the Early Jurassic. Their span encompassed the Middle and Late Jurassic

Epochs, and a few members were present until nearly the end of the age of dinosaurs.

This chapter investigates the traits, lifestyles, and members of the sauropods that thrived during the Middle and Late Jurassic, the heyday of the largest herbivorous dinosaurs.

## EVOLUTION OF THE SAUROPODS

Sauropods evolved separately from the "prosauropods," although both clades are considered part of the Sauropodomorpha and therefore shared a common ancestor. The "prosauropods" did not achieve the enormous sizes seen in the sauropods and maintained a basic body plan that grew to no more than about 35 feet (10.5 m) in the largest species. Most "prosauropods" were extinct by the beginning of the Middle Jurassic, the same general time during which sauropods were beginning to diversify and radiate with great success. It has been presumed that the success of sauropods probably played a role in the demise of the "prosauropods"; sauropods edged them out of the middle to high browsing ranges of available vegetation and competed them out of existence.

Fossil evidence of the earliest sauropods is fragmentary, but even the best known of the earliest sauropods were already geographically widespread by the end of the Early Jurassic. Evidence of **basal** sauropods has been found in Africa, Asia, Europe, and possibly North America and South America.

The earliest known sauropod is *Antetonitrus* (Late Triassic, South Africa) dating from 220 million to 215 million years ago. Measuring between 26 and 33 feet (8 to 10 m) long, *Antetonitrus* was a **transitional** form between the common ancestor of "prosauropods" and sauropods. It had some of the features found in "prosauropods," such as a grasping claw on its front feet, and legs and feet that had not yet been optimized like the weight-bearing limbs of later sauropods. The dinosaur is known from a single specimen, probably that of a juvenile, consisting primarily of limb, foot, and vertebral elements. The skull is not yet known. *Antetonitrus* was

*Apatosaurus* herd and *Ceratosaurus*

identified and named by British paleontologist Adam Yates and South African paleontologist James Kitching (1922–2003). The name *Antetonitrus*, given by Kitching, means "before the thunder," acknowledging this sauropod as an ancestor of the so-called earth-shaking giants to follow.

Other noteworthy early sauropods—including *Blikanasaurus* (Late Triassic, Lesotho); *Gongxianosaurus* (Early Jurassic, China); *Kotasaurus* (Early Jurassic, India); *Vulcanodon* (Early Jurassic, Zimbabwe); and *Tazoudasaurus* (Early Jurassic, Morocco)—continued the trend in sauropod evolution toward quadrupedal gigantism. Among the anatomical innovations advanced by these early sauropods were **forelimbs** that were becoming longer, an upper-**hind-limb** bone (**femur**) that was straighter and longer than the lower leg bone (**tibia**), four fused **sacral vertebrae**, and a general trend toward a rounded, more U-shaped snout and jaw with plucking and piercing teeth.

## SAUROPOD TRAITS

The anatomical features of sauropods that made them a unique clade of dinosaurs revolved around two aspects of their lifestyle: a tendency toward gigantism and their vegetarian diet. Most of the **diagnostic traits**, or features, of sauropod skeletons are adaptations that improved their ability to grow large and to eat and metabolize huge quantities of plants.

All sauropods had a generally similar body plan. It featured a small head, a long neck, quadrupedal posture, and a long tail. This is not to suggest, however, that all sauropods were basically the same. There was significant variation among different groups of sauropods, which resulted in highly distinguishable anatomical features of the skulls, vertebrae, and limbs.

The most prominent anatomical traits that identify members of the sauropods include the following.

*Forelimbs and hind limbs provided strength and mobility.* The proportions, bone shapes, flexibility, and joint structures found in the legs of sauropods were significantly different from those of "prosauropods" and theropods. One telltale sign of a sauropod was that the femur was straighter and longer than the tibia—one of the many limb adaptations that enabled the bearing of great weight yet allowed the animals to move about with relative ease. Quadrupedal movement also required that the front legs be nearly the same length as the hind limbs. In one group of sauropods, the brachiosaurs, this trend resulted in forelimbs that were longer than the hind limbs, an advantage that allowed these largest of the sauropods to reach even higher into trees with their long necks.

*Four or more sacral vertebrae.* Sauropods had four or more sacral vertebrae, the fused backbones that anchored the pelvic structure

*Apatosaurus* (bones of forelimbs exposed)

that supported the hind limbs. "Prosauropods" before them only had three sacral vertebrae. Sacral vertebrae provided a rigid connection to strengthen the pelvic and hind limb structure and improved the ability of the skeleton to support great weight.

*Strong, weight-bearing feet.* The treelike limbs of sauropods were supported by feet with large, robust toes and claws. The first, or inside, digit of each foot—in the same position as the human big toe—was weight bearing and reinforced by an especially large and deep claw on the **ungual**. There was a marked reduction in the size of the unguals from the inside to outside toes, making the limbs into veritable columns: compact yet sturdily built weight-bearing structures. The ankle bones of sauropods were not fused or ossified, providing flexion while the animals walked.

*Elongation of the neck.* The gradual elongation of the neck marked one of the hallmarks of sauropod evolution. With longer necks, these giants increased the reach of their heads to the sides in some species and to greater heights in others, presumably to improve the efficiency of gathering food.

*Skulls, nostrils, and teeth.* The so-called "business end" of the sauropod was the head, where it took in vegetation to nourish its enormous body. Generally speaking, sauropods had small heads in comparison to the sizes of their bodies. The jaws had a U-shaped curvature at the snout instead of the sharper, nearly pointed snouts of theropods and most "prosauropods." Sauropod teeth were adapted for plucking and stripping vegetation from branches rather than chewing it. The skulls of sauropods conformed to three basic shapes: long and slender with elongate snouts, short and broad with abrupt snouts, and a version that was somewhat in between these two extremes. There was a gradual shift in the position of nostrils from the front of the snout, as in most other animals, to a position higher up on the top of the skull. In later sauropods, such as the brachiosaurids and diplodocids, the nostrils had migrated well up on the skull, either in front of or between the eyes on top of the skull. All of these features of the sauropod skull are diagnostic at various taxonomic levels and will be discussed in greater detail below.

## Sauropod Groups

The fossil record of sauropods is generous, but their enormous size produced a bias in the fossil record against the preservation of complete specimens. More than 90 genera of sauropod dinosaurs have been validated by scientific scrutiny, and another 30 or more genera have been proposed but not generally accepted due to the lack of enough diagnostic fossil material. Of the 90 valid genera, only about 22 have been based on the remains of the skull as well as other skeletal parts of the body. The biggest and bulkiest bones of sauropods are typically represented largely by their thick and robust limb bones, which are more commonly found in the fossil record than other, smaller and more fragile body parts. It is fair to say that, given a choice, paleontologists would gladly trade the effort needed to recover several large limb bones for one good skull or jaw. Such is the nature of digging up the bones of sauropods.

Sauropods maintained a remarkably consistent body plan and often tended toward gigantism throughout their history, from the earliest members of the clade in the Late Triassic to the relatively few surviving lines at the end of the days of the dinosaurs. That sauropods existed in one form or another for a span of about 163 million years is astounding in itself. That they lasted for so long with relatively few major changes in their overall body plan is noteworthy for such a large group of animals. Despite the superficial resemblance among taxa, however, sauropods exhibited great diversity at the level of individual genera.

The fragmentary nature of the sauropod fossil record for many years made it difficult to ascertain these creatures' closest evolutionary relationships. A spate of discoveries in the past 20 years and a dedicated new generation of researchers have done much to correct this. British paleontologist Paul Upchurch and American paleontologist Jeffrey Wilson have each recently conducted detailed **cladistic analysis** of sauropods. The result of their work has been a better breakdown of groups within the sauropods, based on shared traits within a given clade. The sauropod groups described in the text that follows are based on their work as of 2004.

Sauropods are divided into three smaller groups as shown in the figure "Dinosaur Clades and Relationships: Sauropoda," which depicts the evolutionary relationships of the Sauropodomorpha.

The most primitive members of this clade are known as basal sauropoda and include such dinosaurs as *Blikanasaurus* and *Vulcanodon*, which lived during the Late Triassic and Early Jurassic. These animals are described in detail in another book in this series, *Dawn of the Dinosaur Age*.

*Eusauropoda.* This is a group of somewhat primitive sauropods whose traits still resembled those of basal sauropods more than

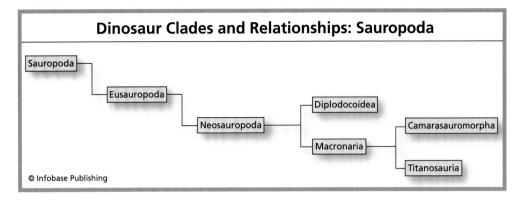

Dinosaur Clades and Relationships: Sauropoda

later, more advanced taxa. The eusauropods lived from the Early Jurassic to Late Jurassic. Notable adaptations shared by taxa in this clade include a broad, rounded snout; the placement of the nostrils more toward the top of the skull—a trait also found in neosauropods and macronarians; an increased number of cervical vertebrae, sometimes resulting in an extremely long neck; a trend toward lighter, more sculpted vertebrae; and weight-supporting modifications to the feet, limbs, pelvis, and ankles. Eusauropods are known from nine genera for which there is adequate diagnostic fossil material. Some of the best-known eusauropods are *Shunosaurus* (Middle Jurassic, China); *Omeisaurus* (Middle Jurassic, China); *Patagosaurus* (Middle Jurassic, Argentina); and the very long-necked *Mamenchisaurus* (Late Jurassic, China).

*Neosauropoda.* These sauropods make up the largest number of taxa and certainly the most famous. Among them are the longest (*Diplodocus*), tallest (*Brachiosaurus*), and heaviest (*Argentinosaurus*) of the sauropodomorphs, as well as the most complete specimen (*Camarasaurus*) and the animal with the longest neck—40 feet (12 m)—of any known vertebrate (*Sauroposeidon*). Living from the Middle Jurassic to Early Cretaceous, neosauropods continued to evolve traits to improve their weight-bearing capacity and size; these traits included the lengthening of the neck by the inclusion of 12 or more cervical vertebrae; pillarlike limbs; modified pelvic, ankle, and foot bones; and continued development of less bulky vertebrae. The Neosauropoda are further divided into two groups, the Diplodocoidea and the Macronaria, each of which includes smaller clades:

*Diplodocoidea.* This clade includes lengthy, somewhat slender animals with a long, narrow skull, a boxlike snout, and peg-like teeth. The nostrils had migrated to the top of the skull and were positioned just in front of the eyes. The Diplodocoidea had whiplike tails, and their limbs showed a reduction in ankle and foot bones. Members of the Diplodocoidea also had elaborately carved and hollowed vertebrae that lightened their weight while making space for vital blood vessels and possibly for air sacs, as in birds, to be used in respiration and cooling.

*Rebbachisauridae.* Several genera are known in this clade. The rebbachisaurids ranged in what was the Southern Hemisphere of the Mesozoic Era, and at least one **taxon** is known from the Northern Hemisphere (Spain). These sauropods lacked the V-shaped **neural spines** on their vertebrae and the forked **chevrons** that are found in other members of the Diplodocoidea. Some taxa had spines on their backs. Rebbachisaurids include *Nigersaurus* (Early Cretaceous, North Africa); *Rayosaurus* (Early to Late Cretaceous, Argentina); *Rebbachisaurus* (Early Cretaceous, Morocco); *Limaysaurus* (Early Cretaceous, Argentina); *Cathartesaura* (Late Cretaceous, Argentina); and possibly *Amazonsaurus* (Early Cretaceous, Brazil).

*Dicraeosauridae.* This branch of the Diplodocoidea includes three genera. Dicraeosaurids had shorter necks and long spines on their vertebrae that may have supported skin-covered fins or sails. Dicraeosaurids are known from partial skeletons including some skull material. The two genera are *Dicraeosaurus* (Late Jurassic, Tanzania) and *Amargasaurus* (Early Cretaceous, Argentina).

*Diplodocidae.* This clade comprises eight genera and is well known from some exquisite specimens, particularly those of

*Amargasaurus*

*Diplodocus.* These large dinosaurs had forked chevrons on their spines. Their skulls were somewhat flat on top, with their nostrils facing skyward. They had 70 to 80 tail vertebrae. Current thinking is that the necks of this taxon were not flexible enough to be lifted high for treetop browsing, making these dinosaurs grazers and browsers of low- to middle-height flora, extending their necks over a horizontal plane about level with the shoulders. The known genera of diplodocids include *Diplodocus* (Late Jurassic, Utah, Wyoming, New Mexico, and Colorado); *Apatosaurus* (Late Jurassic, Colorado, Wyoming, Oklahoma, and Utah); *Barosaurus* (Late Jurassic, South Dakota and Utah); *Australodocus* (Late Jurassic, Tanzania); *Dinheirosaurus* (Late Jurassic, Portugal); *Cetiosauriscus* (Middle to Late Jurassic, England); *Supersaurus* (Late Jurassic, Colorado); and *Eobrontosaurus* (Late Jurassic, Colorado and Wyoming). A large specimen of *Diplodocus,* and previously identified as *Seismosaurus,* is known from a pelvis and partial vertebral column and is thought to have been the longest dinosaur, at a possible 110 feet (33 m) long.

*Macronaria.* This subgroup of the Neosauropoda is distinguished by skull features that include a nasal opening that was larger than

*Apatosaurus*

the eye opening. In contrast to the Diplodocoidea, macronarians were generally larger, taller, and bulkier but shorter sauropods.

*Camarasauridae.* This clade comprises one **genus**. These bulky sauropods had a boxy skull with broadly spoon-shaped teeth and nostrils elevated high on the top of the skull that faced outward rather than upward. Members of this taxon include *Camarasaurus* (Late Jurassic, Colorado, Wyoming, and Utah).

*Brachiosauridae.* Three genera make up this clade. The tallest and some of the bulkiest sauropods belong to the Brachiosauridae. They were distinguished by forelimbs that were longer than their hind limbs, and by long necks. These spectacular animals included *Brachiosaurus* (Late Jurassic, Tanzania and Colorado); *Cedarosaurus* (Early Cretaceous, Utah); and *Sauroposeidon* (Early Cretaceous, Oklahoma).

Long considered the largest and tallest sauropods, the Brachiosauridae were named for *Brachiosaurus*, a partial first specimen discovered in Colorado in 1909 by Elmer S. Riggs (1869–1963). The dinosaur became much better understood after the unearthing of five partial skeletons in Tanzania between 1909 and 1912. The African expeditionary force was supervised by German Werner Janensch (1878–1969) for the Humboldt

*Brachiosaurus*

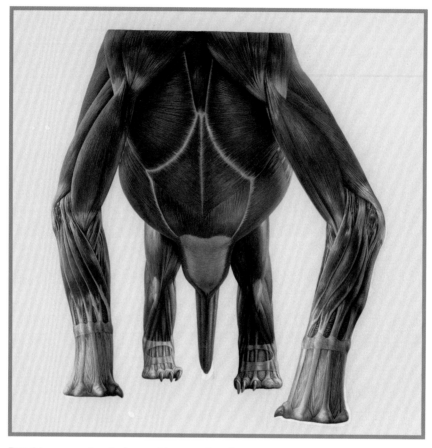

*Brachiosaurus* forelimbs and torso, showing muscles

Museum of Natural History in Berlin and to this date ranks as one of the most elaborate dinosaur digs ever mounted, based on the number of people engaged in the work (400 to 500 African workers per season); the geographic area of the dig (2 square miles/5 square km); the quantity of fossils (250 tons/225 metric tons); and the number of specimens (almost 100 **articulated skeletons** and hundreds of separate bones). Among the prizes were enough partial skeletons of *Brachiosaurus* to mount an extraordinary composite individual that still serves as the centerpiece of the main exhibit hall of the Humboldt Museum.

*Brachiosaurus* digestive system

This specimen is the largest mounted dinosaur skeleton in the world.

*Brachiosaurus* could reach upward of 53 feet (16 m), making it one of the tallest of dinosaurs. The heavyweight title for the bulkiest of dinosaurs now goes to another group of macronarians, the titanosaurs, a clade of mostly Cretaceous sauropods described in *Last of the Dinosaurs.*

*Titanosauria.* This large clade, predominantly of the Southern Hemisphere, comprises 29 reliably known genera. The last of the sauropods were titanosaurs. Their largest members included the heaviest land animals ever to grace the Earth. The **sacrum** consisted of six vertebrae. The hind limbs of titanosaurs were spread more widely than those of other sauropods. The front limbs were reduced in length but supported by an oversized scapula. Titanosaur feet were small. The spines of the backbone were divided by a deep cleft. The tail was short, and

Cross-section of *Brachiosaurus* gut in which food slowly fermented

the neck was robust and directed upward. Some titanosaurs had extremely long necks, as evidenced by the recently discovered *Erketu* (Early Cretaceous, Mongolia), whose neck was nearly 30 feet (9 m) long.

Titanosaurs are also known from opposite ends of the size scale. A diminutive species discovered in Germany and named in 2006 has become the smallest known adult specimen of a sauropod: *Europasaurus* (Late Jurassic, Germany) was a dwarf species whose maximum length was about 20 feet (6.2 m). In contrast, the heaviest of all dinosaurs was also a titanosaur:

*Argentinosaurus* (Early Cretaceous, Argentina) is known from only a partial skeleton but appears to have been the mast massive of dinosaurs, weighing upward of 99 tons (90 metric tons) and measuring about 100 feet (30 m) long. Other members of the titanosaurs have been found in widely distant geographic locations and include *Chubutisaurus* (Early Cretaceous, Argentina); *Huabeisaurus* (Late Cretaceous, China); *Janenschia* (Late Jurassic, Tanzania); *Phuwiangosaurus* (Early Cretaceous, Thailand); *Alamosaurus* (Late Cretaceous, New Mexico, Utah, and Texas); *Antarctosaurus* (Late Cretaceous, Argentina, Chile, and Uruguay); *Malawisaurus* (Early Cretaceous, Malawi); *Paralititan* (Late Cretaceous, Egypt); *Rapetosaurus* (Late Cretaceous, Madagascar); and *Isisaurus* (Late Cretaceous, India). *Nemegtosaurus* (Late Cretaceous, Mongolia) and *Quaesitosaurus* (Late Cretaceous, Mongolia), once thought to be diplodocids, are now considered titanosaurs that exhibited some convergent evolution with diplodocids.

## SAUROPOD LIFESTYLES

Fragmentary remains of the sauropod *Cetiosaurus* (Middle Jurassic, England) were on hand when British paleontologist Sir Richard Owen coined the name "Dinosauria" in 1842; however, Owen thought the bones were from a huge, extinct marine crocodile, so they were not a component in his original conception of a "dinosaur." Spare parts of sauropods continued to be discovered for the next 30 years, but none revealed the true size and spectacular nature of these giants. The dearth of knowledge about sauropods changed in a flash when the search for dinosaurs picked up in the American West in the 1870s. A spectacular series of Late Jurassic dinosaur discoveries in Colorado and Wyoming revealed a hitherto unknown dinosaur ecosystem and some of the most complete specimens of sauropod giants ever discovered.

The rush to discover dinosaurs in the American West was led by two competing paleontologists from the Northeast: Edward Drinker Cope of Philadelphia and Othniel Charles Marsh of New

Haven, Connecticut. Among the puzzles they sought to unravel was the lifestyle of the giant herbivorous sauropods.

British paleontologist John Phillips (1800–1874) preceded Cope and Marsh in speculating about the lifestyles of sauropods. In 1871, after studying a well-preserved partial specimen of *Cetiosaurus*, Phillips concluded that the sturdy limbs of the dinosaur strongly suggested that it was a fully terrestrial beast. By 1878, after Cope and Marsh had discovered several astoundingly complete sauropod specimens—including *Camarasaurus* and *Apatosaurus*—the two Americans came to the same conclusion as Phillips. As they continued to scrape away at the blocks of fossils to reveal the finer details of these dinosaurs, however, certain anatomical features persuaded Cope and Marsh that a terrestrial lifestyle may not have been possible for these heaviest of animals. Among the fossil clues that changed their minds were the placement of nostrils on the tops of the skulls, the long necks, and nonchewing teeth that the men perceived as "weak." Cope and Marsh concluded that sauropods were probably semiaquatic animals that lived in the water to support their great weight. The long neck and nostrils on top of the skull were viewed as the dinosaurian equivalent of a snorkel, to be used for breathing air while the animal's body was almost fully submerged. The teeth seemed capable of grasping only soft-bodied plants.

By 1878, Cope had sketched an illustration of several *Camarasaurus* fully submerged in the water, eating plants from the bottom and lifting their heads to get a gulp of air. Marsh agreed with this interpretation. He wrote in 1895 that "In habits *Brontosaurus* was more or less amphibious, and its food was probably aquatic plants or other succulent vegetation."

Once established, the view of sauropods as semiaquatic creatures was difficult to refute. It stuck for nearly 100 years, despite several reasoned arguments to the contrary. The case for aquatic sauropods began to crumble for good in 1951, when British mammal paleontologist Kenneth Kermack demonstrated that the idea of deep-water sauropods defied the laws of physics. A sauropod

Edward Drinker Cope

submerged up to its head in water would find it impossible to take a breath due to the effects of extreme water pressure on the lungs and the base of the neck, where the muscles for respiration are located in vertebrates.

Despite Kermack's assertions to the contrary, the concept of amphibious sauropods persisted into the 1960s, in academic textbooks as well as the popular press. The case for terrestrial sauropods finally began to gain widespread acceptance due to the innovative paleontological work of American Robert Bakker. In 1971—

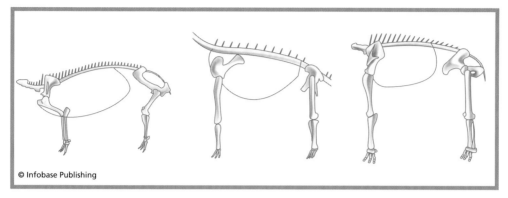

Bakker compared the body shapes of hippos (*left*), apatosaur dinosaurs (*center*), and elephants (*right*) to help prove that dinosaurs were mostly terrestrial animals (after Bakker, 1971).

precisely 100 years after Phillips first suggested that sauropods were most likely terrestrial—Bakker published a provocative study that provided more than enough reasons to release sauropods from the water once and for all. His reasons included the following.

- Nostrils placed high on the skull were not a compelling argument for a snorkel-like function. Many **extant** lizards have large nostrils high on the skull, and those nostrils are not used as snorkels.
- Aquatic vertebrates usually have flattened tails to aid in swimming; in contrast, the tails of some sauropods were long, whiplike, and useless for propelling a sauropod through the water.
- Sauropod teeth show tooth wear and abrasion that would not be present if the animals ate only soft aquatic plants.
- Similarly, a lack of flat, grinding tooth surfaces in the sauropod mouth was not a convincing argument for a diet of soft aquatic plants. Sauropods could ingest tough vegetation and digest it in the large fermenting chambers of the gut.
- Sauropods had a deep body shape similar to that found in extant terrestrial quadrupeds such as the elephant. Modern

amphibious animals such as the hippopotamus have round body forms not found in the sauropods.

- The vertebral column of a sauropod was well adapted to support the animal's large body weight on land. In particular, the shapes of sauropod vertebrae provide many sculpted surfaces and spines for the attachment of muscles.
- The rigid and straight legs of sauropods are characteristic of animals adapted for walking on land.
- Sauropods had closely spaced toes to provide sure footing, in contrast to the widely spread toes of aquatic animals that tread in areas where gaining a foothold is less necessary.
- Tall animals tend to be tree browsers. While not all sauropods were adapted for high browsing, many were.

Although somewhat speculative, Bakker's compelling arguments nonetheless withstood the critical review of other paleontologists and turned the tide in favor of a terrestrial lifestyle for the sauropods. This is not to say that sauropods never ventured into the water, but that they were predominantly adapted for a life on dry land.

The success of Bakker's study of sauropods sparked a renaissance in the study of dinosaur behavior, encouraging paleontologists to broaden their investigation of dinosaurs beyond the dimensions of fossil bones.

## Sauropod Feeding

Bakker made a convincing case for a terrestrial lifestyle of the sauropods. One aspect of his circumstantial evidence supporting sauropod life out of water was his assessment of where sauropod fossils have been found. Sauropod bones have been discovered all over the globe and often, as in the rich Morrison Formation fossil beds of Colorado and Wyoming, in deposits that were once part of vast floodplains, "not lakes and swamps," as Bakker reminds us. A floodplain is an expanse of open land surrounding a river that experiences periodic and sudden seasonal flooding. In the Morrison

Formation, these floodplains were dry and often arid environments, home to the kinds of vigorous evergreen plants that were widespread in Jurassic times. Given a terrestrial lifestyle, the next vital link in understanding just how sauropods lived is to examine their adaptations for eating conifers and other kinds of plants that were abundant in their ecosystem.

The climate, terrain, and aridity of the sauropod habitat were similar to what the African elephant experiences today. It was a warm world with seasonal dry spells interrupted by shorter periods of torrential rain. **Trackway** evidence for herding sauropods suggests that the animals migrated, possibly to follow food supplies, because a large herd of sauropods could deplete available vegetation quickly. A herd would need to move continually to find more food and to give the just-vacated herbivory a chance to recover. Sauropods may even have returned to familiar eating sites, perhaps as part of a cyclical migratory route to and from nesting grounds.

The size and body plan of the sauropods strongly suggest that they ranged from being low grazers to medium- and high-browsing herbivores, feeding from ground cover in some species and from tree branches in others. The kinds of plants they ate included conifers (evergreens), tree ferns, ginkgo trees, and taller cycads—all examples of hearty, tough vegetation. The grazing and low-browsing diplodocoids almost certainly also fed on shrubby ferns, cycads, and horsetails, not just trees. Conifers are cone-bearing, woody seed plants. They generally have straight trunks and can reach heights of 330 feet (100 m) in the most robust species. Today's conifers typically have long, needlelike leaves. Some Jurassic varieties, resembling the modern Norfolk Island pine and "monkey puzzle" tree, had long, drooping branches from which close-knit, scalelike leaves grew directly from the limbs, without branches. Ginkgo trees, which also survive to this day, are another form of tree with branches and broad, fan-shaped leaves. These examples of probable sauropod food were hardly moist and succulent. Obtaining nutrition from them would have required some specialized adaptations for gathering the leaves and extracting the maximum amount of nutrition from them.

### Sauropod Skulls and Teeth

The teeth and skulls of sauropods varied little over the long course of their evolution. Even the earliest sauropods had a tendency for large bodies and developed jaws and teeth for plucking and stripping leaves from vegetation. The significance of such teeth becomes dramatically apparent when they are compared to the teeth of mammals, even humans. The mammal mouth is **heterodont**: It has teeth of many different shapes, with each shape adapted for a particular job during the process of eating. Some teeth are good at stabbing; others at plucking or shredding food; still others are better for chewing food. What most mammals have in common is a set of ridged or bumpy grinding teeth that form a relatively continuous surface, plus a jaw that allows the lower jaw to move in directions other than just up and down for grinding food between the upper and lower jaws. Chewing or grinding food in the mouth mechanically breaks it down and begins the process of releasing nutrients from food cells. The chewing of food in the mouth makes the food easier to digest when it reaches the bacteria and enzyme bath of the stomach.

Sauropods never evolved grinding teeth. This may seem unimaginable for animals that were the largest plant eaters of all time. The reason for this may lie in their tremendous size. Chewing food in the mouth takes time that may have been better spent obtaining more food to nourish such giants. Instead, sauropods achieved the task of eating through an innovative yet elegantly simple process. They plucked or stripped food, such as pine needles and ginkgo leaves, from tree branches with their teeth and swallowed bunches of it whole. From the mouth, food was swallowed down the long esophagus and fed into a huge fermentation chamber in the gut that slowly extracted nutrients from ingested food. One paleontologist who has devoted much time to understanding the digestive process of sauropods is American James Farlow. He pictured a large fermentation chamber beyond the stomach where gastric juices consisting of help-ful bacteria did the work of breaking down plant cells and releasing nutrients into the blood stream of the dinosaur.

In retrospect, the simple eating process of sauropods seems to have been ideally suited to their enormous energy requirements. Having such a fermentation chamber in a large animal makes good sense because plant matter sits in the gut longer, allowing more nutrients to be extracted. Sauropods did not have to eat voraciously to get enough nutrients. In comparison to smaller animals, just being big enabled sauropods to get more out of the food they ate. Considering their size and the type of food they ate, sauropods probably processed food slowly along a long gut in order to maxi-mize nutrient extraction.

Sauropod skulls were small in comparison with their bodies. The jaws of most known sauropods were specialized for shearing, plucking, or stripping vegetation from branches. There was a trend in sauropod skulls for the external nostril opening to be on the top, or dorsal, surface of the skull, in front of and above the eyes. The reason for a dorsally positioned nostril is not entirely understood; it has become a sauropod puzzle in need of a solution. Whales have blowholes on the tops of their skulls so that they can inhale and exhale while partially submerged. Sauropods were not water-dwelling creatures, however, so the topside position of the nostrils cannot be attributed to a snorkel-like purpose.

Among extant terrestrial animals, both the elephant and the tapir have nostrils on top of the skull as well as a trunk—a mus-cular extension of the lips that the animal uses like a fifth limb to grasp food. Sketches of sauropods with trunks are more fantasy, however; sauropods, like other reptiles, very likely did not possess the kinds of facial muscles needed to operate a trunk. What can be said about sauropod nostrils, however, is that they were overly big. In addition, the sauropod nostril may have been surrounded by a fleshy, bulbous chamber, providing a resonator through which these dinosaurs could have projected nose sounds. Bakker has lov-ingly called the nostrils of sauropods "nose flutes," and this idea

*Aucasaurus* attacking titanosaur nests

cannot be entirely dismissed. Another reason to have a large nasal cavity would have been to improve the animals' sense of smell—a highly valuable advantage for sauropods, which shared their world with extra-large predators equipped to bring them down. Being able to smell an approaching predator would have given sauropods a chance to flee or take a defensive stance, whichever they may have preferred. A highly placed nostril may also have given sauropods an additional advantage while eating, keeping the nose out of the way of the animal's snout as it repeatedly and systematically reached into trees to strip vegetation.

Different sauropod clades evolved several variations on the shapes of the skull and jaws. Most sauropods had four premaxillary teeth. Early eusauropods, such as *Shunosaurus*, exhibited the most primitive sauropod jaw morphology. Their snouts were long and deep, and their teeth were positioned in long rows of 21 teeth in the upper and lower jaws. Evidence of extensive tooth wear in eusauropods shows that their bite was scissorlike and could shear vegetation from branches.

Among the more advanced neosauropods were several variations on the sauropod skull. Basal macronarians, such as *Camarasaurus,* had taller skulls with enormous nostrils and large, spoon-shaped teeth. The bite was more muscular than that of other neosauropods, but the eating strategy was similar in that the teeth could pull, pluck, and shear leaves from tree branches.

Brachiosaurs had longer snouts than *Camarasaurus* and enlarged nasal openings atop their skulls, in front of and between the eyes. Brachiosaur teeth were long and less spoonlike than those of camarasaurs. The crown of the tooth was rounded but usually showed flattening due to tooth wear. The sides of brachiosaur teeth had long, rounded ridges. Brachiosaurs probably used a plucking and stripping action to pull food into the mouth.

Arguably the most advanced and efficient sauropod skull and jaw morphologies were those of the diplodocids. The teeth of these sauropods were clustered at the fronts of their long snouts and were distinctively peglike and unadorned. When closed, the jaws allowed the teeth to overlap in such a way as to form an effective rake for stripping leaves from branches. One can picture a diplodocids eating by placing its jaws over the middle of a branch and then raking leaves into its mouth by pulling its head away from the tree. The best-known skulls of titanosaurs, the last of the great line of sauropods, also have peglike teeth but a taller and possibly more muscular jaw. In most respects, the titanosaurs probably had eating habits more like those of diplodocids than like those of other lines of sauropods. There are some as-yet-unpublished skull specimens of titanosaurs, however, that have brachiosaur/camarasaur-style teeth. Other titanosaurs, such as *Malawisaurus,* have teeth that are somewhat in between the peglike and spoonlike shapes of other sauropod teeth. All titanosaurs cannot be painted with the same brush; there appear to have been different feeding styles within the group.

The forelimbs and necks of sauropods also figured importantly in their eating habits. It is presumed that their great size made all sauropods middle and high browsers, encouraging comparisons to the giraffe. Only the brachiosaurs, however, with forelimbs that were longer than their hind limbs, come close to the giraffe model. *Brachiosaurus* was indeed a towering browser and the tallest of all dinosaurs, as its limb and neck anatomy attest. Other taxa of sauropods, however, had shorter forelimbs and neck anatomy that was not always suited for flexing vertically.

The **anatomy** of sauropod necks provides many clues to the flexibility and reach of the animals' heads. In 1999, paleontologists Kent Stevens and J. Michael Parrish used three-dimensional computer modeling to simulate the maximum vertical and horizontal head movement possible in *Diplodocus* and *Apatosaurus*, two dinosaurs known from excellent specimens. Stevens and Parrish concluded that diplodocids were able to move their heads in wide horizontal sweeps somewhat low to the ground, but that raising their heads high was virtually impossible due to the inflexibility of their neck vertebrae for vertical movement. A less flexible neck, such as that of the diplodocids, is also presumed for their close relatives, the dicraeosaurids, which also happen to have dorsally placed spines on the base of their necks to add to the inflexibility.

Not all sauropod experts agree with the computer model. Paul Upchurch notes that the four vertebrae at the base of the neck of *Diplodocus* have a ball-and-socket morphology that would have added increased vertical flexibility. Even so, other kinds of evidence regarding diplodocids, including jaw mechanics and tooth shape, strongly hint at a low- to medium-browsing animal, so there is general agreement that diplodocids probably ate at somewhat lower levels of the flora than did other sauropods. Types of sauropods that may have had better vertical reach included some eusauropods, camarasaurs, brachiosaurs, and titanosaurs.

## Dinosaur Physiology and Metabolism

An understanding of dinosaur metabolism would say much about the lifestyles and behaviors of these extinct creatures. Metabolism is the combination of all biochemical processes that take place in an organism to keep it alive. The metabolic processes within a living animal encompass such things as respiration, food intake and digestion, growth rate, body temperature, pulmonary functions, and other systems. Understanding the metabolism of dinosaurs is a challenge because none of the soft tissues, body fluids, and organic matter (other than bones and teeth) are usually fossilized. Not surprisingly, since the earliest discoveries of dinosaurs, there has been an active debate over their metabolism.

From the early history of dinosaur science, there has been a tendency to characterize these creatures as being either **ectothermic** (cold-blooded) and reptilelike or **endothermic** (warm-blooded) like mammals and birds. Consistently, however, dinosaurs have defied convention because they were neither reptiles like crocodiles nor entirely like mammals and birds. Complicating an understanding of their **physiology** were the wide range of dinosaur body sizes and growth rates, the evolutionary divergence of major groups of dinosaurs, and the uniformly warm environments in which they lived. Short of having a living, breathing dinosaur whose temperature one could take, there is no absolute way of determining ectothermic and endothermic metabolism from fossils alone. The debate over dinosaur physiology has therefore taken place along several related—and often circumstantial—lines, including evidence based on the study of the creatures' fossil bones and factors related to the animals' ecology.

### Thermoregulation

The existence of sauropods naturally raises many questions about the physiology and metabolism of the largest of all terrestrial vertebrates. One key to the metabolism and activity level of an animal is the regulation of its body temperature. Among vertebrates, reptiles (lizards, snakes, turtles, and crocodylians), amphibians (frogs and salamanders), and fishes are typically ectothermic, or "cold-blooded." Mammals and birds are typically endothermic, or "warm-blooded." A third thermoregulatory strategy, called **homeothermy**, is also of interest in discussing dinosaurs.

These forms of thermoregulation are defined as follows:

*Ectothermy (cold-bloodedness).* Some animals derive their heat from external sources. The body temperature of an ectotherm is approximately that of the surrounding environment, but the animal may actually become warmer than the air temperature while basking in full sun. Cold-blooded creatures are usually less active in colder weather and at night, when sunlight is unavailable.

*Endothermy (warm-bloodedness).* Animals whose bodies use this strategy create their own body heat and have a constant body temperature without regard to their surroundings. The activity level of an endotherm can remain constant in warm or cold weather as long as it has food to power the metabolism, and, if the animal is small, some means of controlling heat loss, such as fur or feathers.

*Homeothermy (ability to maintain a near-constant body temperature).* Large-bodied animals retain heat due to their large size. The internal core temperature of a homeotherm is affected by its size, or body mass. Among crocodylians and sea turtles, for example, larger individuals lose heat much more slowly than smaller ones; once those larger individuals attain a certain temperature, they stay at that temperature longer. Body heat comes from their surroundings as well as from the energy created by the digestion of food. The same might have been true for some of the larger dinosaurs. **Gigantothermy** is a form of homeothermy that combines low metabolic rate with large size and the way in which blood is circulated outwardly to body tissues.

The longstanding concepts of ectothermy and endothermy have proved to be much more complex than once thought. In contrast to the now-outmoded definitional concepts of "cold-" and "warm-bloodedness," it is now understood that multiple metabolic processes are acting in tandem to produce any particular type of metabolism; and these processes do not fall neatly into clearly defined categories. Nature proves more diverse and difficult to quantify than the human mind, with its love for categorization, can always grasp.

Also coming into play are contrasts between homeothermy and **poikilothermy** (the ability to regulate and maintain a temperature) and **tachymetabolism** versus **bradymetabolism** (fast or slow resting metabolic processes). Naked mole rats, bats, and hummingbirds are endothermic and homeothermic but bradymetabolic: They slow their metabolisms down when resting to conserve energy. Stereotypical endotherms such as mammals and birds do not do this. Are they "warm-blooded"? Similarly, tuna are ectothermic but homeothermic: They are able to maintain a higher body temperature than the surrounding water but without generating the heat themselves. Are they "cold-blooded"?

Non-avian dinosaurs ranged in all sizes, from smaller than a chicken to large-bodied forms that approached the probable limits of terrestrial animal size. Most paleontologists once assumed that dinosaurs were lethargic, slow moving, and stereotypically ectothermic—like their reptilian ancestors, and exemplified by a lizard. The behavior of dinosaurs was likened to that of overgrown crocodiles.

Beginning in 1972, paleontologist Robert Bakker began to advocate that endothermy was present in all dinosaurs. His reasons were based on his interpretation of their anatomy as indicating that they were active, lively creatures, as well as on ecological factors that he interpreted from the fossil record. In one study analyzing the numbers of predator compared to prey dinosaurs currently known, Bakker argued that the ratio mirrored that of ecosystems made up of extant endotherms. Lauded for creativity but soundly criticized for logical flaws in this analysis—one being that predator-to-prey ratios among ectotherms are not substantively different than among endotherms—Bakker nonetheless raised the volume of debate over dinosaur metabolism to a higher level. He offered other circumstantial evidence for dinosaur endothermy, such as their erect gait (normally seen in endotherms) and mammal- or birdlike microstructure of bones; he predicted the presence of insulating feathers on carnivorous dinosaurs more than 10 years before unequivocal evidence for feathered dinosaurs emerged from China in the late 1990s.

Understanding the metabolic systems of dinosaurs would provide clues to their behavior. If dinosaurs were "cold-blooded," they may have spent much of their time moving in and out of the sun or shade to regulate their body temperature. If they were "warm-blooded," dinosaurs would have been more active, moving about at will, day and night. Having an answer to this question would also help us understand the relationship of dinosaurs to modern animals, such as birds and other reptiles, as well as help us understand what were important factors in their evolution and extinction patterns.

### Metabolic Options for Dinosaurs

One of the major problems for arguing that all dinosaurs were endotherms is that dinosaurs came in small and large sizes. Dinosaurs also evolved along two separate lines—the ornithischians and the saurischians. It is reasonable to assume that these different evolutionary pathways may have resulted in different thermoregulatory adaptations over the millions of years of dinosaur existence. In short, not all dinosaurs necessarily had the same kinds of metabolisms; metabolic rates, like everything else, evolved with time.

Endothermy as currently seen in extant animals would not have been possible in the largest of dinosaurs. Warm-blooded creatures the size of tyrannosaurs and sauropods would have overheated easily, unable to adequately release as much heat energy as they were generating. Being endothermic also would have required an extraordinary amount of food—the fuel source behind the energy of body that becomes heat in an endotherm. It has been calculated that the food requirements of a large sauropod would have been about 40 percent greater than in an equally large ectothermic animal, a requirement that would have been impractical even for a dinosaur. The puzzle facing paleontologists is to explain how sauropods could have been active, terrestrial animals but not endothermic.

The answer lies in the huge size of sauropods. In the late 1940s, American paleontologist Edwin H. Colbert (1905–2001) and his herpetologist colleagues Raymond B. Cowles (1896–1975) and Charles M. Bogert (1908–1992) conducted experiments to test the body temperature tolerances of alligators. Working with a dozen or so live alligators of various sizes, they ran the animals through several exercises on land and in the water and kept a record of their changing body temperatures. What the researchers learned was that the temperature of the largest alligators heated up or cooled down at slower rates than the temperature of the smaller specimens. From this work the team extrapolated a formula, based on body mass, for the regulation of body temperature in ectothermic reptiles.

Colbert, a dinosaur expert, decided to ratchet up the formula to see what would happen if it were applied to ectotherms the size of dinosaurs of various kinds. What he found was that the largest dinosaurs, specifically the sauropods, would have maintained nearly a constant, relatively high body temperature, given their environment. Even without being endothermic, some dinosaurs could have benefited from many of the advantages of warm-bloodedness. A dinosaur with a consistently moderate body temperature also would have required less food than an endothermic animal of the same size. Many follow-up studies by other paleontologists and biological researchers have supported Colbert's realization. The conclusion? Ectotherms can achieve high body temperature and homeothemy by sheer body mass alone, without having to have a warm-blooded metabolism.

Homeothermy relies on a combination of biologic and environmental factors to work.

*A warm, temperate climate, such as that enjoyed by the dinosaurs.* In a large dinosaur, heat absorbed during the day would be retained for many hours past dark.

*Large body size.* The larger the body, the greater its ability to retain heat that was absorbed from the environment or produced internally through normal metabolic processes.

*Layers of body insulation.* Layers of fat and the very large gut of the dinosaurs were probably capable of retaining body heat.

*A digestive process that produces heat.* Ornithopods digested their food using a gastric fermentation process that naturally produced heat as a by-product.

*Special adaptations of the circulatory system.* Blood flow and its circulatory path would be used to pass heat from the core or gut of the dinosaur to its surface, where the heat could safely be shed to avoid overheating. The extensive surface area of the dinosaur body, including the long tail, may have been part of this strategy for shedding excess heat.

*Air sacs.* As noted below, the extensive air-sac systems of theropods and sauropods (though not "prosauropods") would also have functioned as effective heat-dump systems for ridding the animals of excessive body heat.

All of the above reasons made it possible for sauropods and other forms of large dinosaurs to maintain high body temperatures while still having lower, cold-blooded metabolic rates.

Here the outmoded concept of "warm-bloodedness" comes into play: If these animals maintained a high body temperature (homeothermy), doesn't that make them "warm-blooded," even if they were not generating heat internally (endothermy)? (Although they were generating heat internally whether they liked it or not—digestion will do that, especially in an herbivore with a fermenting chamber in its gut—this is *fermentative endothermy.*)

One might next speculate: If sauropods were homeothermic, and so had the benefits of an active metabolism without the burden of having to eat as much as a warm-blooded creature, how much food did they require? A 1997 study by paleontologists Frank V. Paladino, James R. Spotila, and Peter Dodson suggested that a large, homeothermic sauropod could have survived on a daily consumption of about 68 gallons (262 liters) of water and 616 pounds (280 kilograms) of vegetation—a large amount, but a substantially smaller burden than would have been necessary if these dinosaurs had been warm-blooded.

Body mass alone does not determine whether an animal is "cold-blooded" or "warm-blooded." While homeothermy might be assumed for many large dinosaurs, this idea is based on an assumption that dinosaurs must have been "cold-blooded" to begin with, and there is much evidence to suggest that this was not entirely the case. Dinosaurs large and small had rapid growth rates, as shown by the microscopic study of bone growth, which is more like that of mammals and birds. Dinosaur anatomy suggests an active, more highly energized lifestyle, at least in younger individuals. The Mesozoic environments of the dinosaurs may have required seasonal metabolic changes. Moreover, not all dinosaurs were large, so the question remains of how small to medium-sized dinosaurs maintained an evidently high rate of metabolism.

In 1990, American paleontologist James Farlow assessed the evidence and concluded that dinosaurs were likely "intermediate level endotherms" whose metabolic rates probably varied over the course of their life, beginning life as rapidly growing endotherms and gradually changing to homeotherms if their size allowed. Farlow also thought that some medium to large dinosaurs, particularly theropods, may have been more or less "warm-blooded" for their entire lives. Rather than falling into the bipolar trap of having to categorize dinosaurs as only either ectothermic or endothermic, Farlow suggested that perhaps we just think of them as "damn good reptiles"—ones that do not fit the molds of either living reptiles or mammals and birds. In short, the metabolic strategies employed by animals alive today are not necessarily the only possible metabolic strategies. Moreover, not all dinosaurs necessarily employed the same strategies—larger dinosaurs may have had different metabolisms than smaller dinosaurs, and metabolisms certainly evolved through time, too.

The study of dinosaur metabolism continues to cause debate. One of the most reasoned suggestions for considering dinosaurs as intermediate or higher level endotherms comes from paleontologists Kevin Padian and John R. Horner (b. 1946), who turn to evolution as the key. Because there are no "magic bullets" in the fossil bones of vertebrates that indicate the nature of their thermoregulation, Padian and Horner argue that one should follow the physiological traits that separate more **derived**, highly specialized dinosaurs from basal members of the clade. These traits indicate that dinosaurs were evolving a metabolic process more like that of birds and mammals than that of crocodylians, toward higher metabolic rates and faster growth rates, thus making them unique among vertebrates.

## Sauropod Skeletal Innovation and Locomotion

Sauropods were obligatory quadrupeds; that is, they needed all four legs to walk. Their hind limbs were stronger than their fore-limbs and were either longer than the forelimbs or equal to them in length in all but the brachiosaurs, which had a more giraffelike posture. Having shorter forelimbs than hind limbs, great body mass, and relatively inflexible, treelike limbs limited the speeds at which sauropods could walk and run. This is not to suggest that sauropods were not without some quickness of foot. Fossilized sauropod trackways provide information for estimating walking and running speed. Sauropods seem to have typically ambled at 2 to 4 mph (3.3 to 6.7 km/hr). Maximum speeds for brachiosaurs and diplodocids have been calculated between 12 and 18 mph (20 and 30 km/hr), about the speed of a rapid cross-country bicyclist, but they were unlikely to have been able to attain that speed for long periods.

The stances of titanosaurs were upright but somewhat more sprawling than those of other sauropods; this means that titano-saurs' feet were positioned somewhat farther from the midline of the torso. The wider-gauge walk of titanosaurs may have meant that they were slower than other sauropods that had a more upright walking posture.

Bakker and other paleontologists have popularized the image of sauropods rearing back on their hind limbs and using their tails as tripod supports to extend their vertical feeding ranges. Many artists have also illustrated sauropods in this pose, and it is often applied

*(continues on page 78)*

# THINK ABOUT IT

## The Dinosaur Bone Rush in America: 1877–1889

Dinosaur science as we know it today was a new science, with few practitioners, in the nineteenth century. Most fossil experts of the time were trained in other fields, particularly medicine, animal biology, or geology.

Two of the first and most famous paleontologists in America were Edward Drinker Cope and Othniel Charles Marsh. Cope was based in Philadelphia; Marsh was based in New Haven, Connecticut. Both men studied dinosaurs found in the American West in the 1870s and 1880s, a time during which white settlers were encroaching upon lands occupied by the Plains Indians. After several active years of exploring for fossils in person, both Cope and Marsh found even greater success by hiring numerous crews of fossil hunters to collect bones for them.

Cope and Marsh were not the first scientists to search for dinosaur bones. Before Cope and Marsh, however, only a handful of dinosaurs were known, and little was understood about them. When Cope named his first dinosaur in 1866 there were so few known dinosaurs that they still could be counted on the fingers of one's hands. By 1897, after 30 years of exploration, Cope and Marsh had personally added 37 new dinosaurs that still are recognized today. Among them were many familiar names, including *Apatosaurus*, *Stegosaurus*, *Camarasaurus*, *Triceratops*, and *Allosaurus*.

Cope and Marsh were the first paleontologists who organized scientific expeditions for the specific purpose of finding dinosaur bones, and their expeditions perfected methods for digging and protecting fossils that are still used today. Both men also learned the value of popularizing the science of dinosaurs by writing and lecturing to ordinary citizens about these mysterious creatures from the past.

Cope and Marsh spent their early fossil-hunting days exploring deposits known mostly for extinct mammals and fishes. Marsh was first into the field with several expeditions sponsored by Yale University. Marsh's success stirred the jealously of Cope in Philadelphia, and Cope soon followed Marsh westward. Cope explored some of Marsh's own cherished fossil locations and competed with the man from New Haven for the same kinds of strange, never-before-seen mammal bones.

## The Dinosaur Competition Begins

In 1877, the two scientists turned their attention to dinosaurs because of a letter from a teacher working in and around the town of Morrison, Colorado, near Denver. Arthur Lakes had found some unusually large fossil bones. He first wrote a letter to Marsh to find out whether the scientist would be interested in buying them. Marsh was curious, but instead of jumping at the chance, he politely offered to identify the bones if Lakes would send them to him at Yale, in Connecticut. No deal was struck.

Before long, Lakes discovered more bones, including what looked like a gigantic leg. He wrote to Marsh again. Lakes estimated that the total length of the animal to which this leg belonged must have been 60 to 70 feet, a figure that must have sounded unbelievably big at the time. This time Lakes took more direct action. He packed up 10 crates of the bones and shipped them to Marsh at Yale, thereby hoping to ignite the scientist's curiosity and open his wallet. As a fallback, Lakes also sent a few of the spectacular bones to Cope in Philadelphia.

Cope was the first to act. He was delighted at his good fortune but unaware that Marsh had been sent fossils from the same specimen. Cope set to work writing a scientific description of the dinosaur, but the specimen was not his for long.

Finally deciding to answer the letters from Lakes, Marsh took action—and thereby quickly gained the upper hand. Marsh sent a check to Lakes for 100 dollars, on the condition that he also be given the bones that had already been sent to Cope. Unfortunately for Cope, he had not yet paid Lakes for any of the bones. Cope had to pack them up and send them to Marsh in Connecticut. So it was that Othniel C. Marsh identified his first new dinosaur without having set foot out of his office in New Haven. The dinosaur was a sauropod.

*(continues)*

*(continued)*

Marsh hired fossil collectors to work with Lakes and continue digging for every dinosaur they could find in the Colorado deposit. The skeletons that Lakes had found were spectacular. The fossils were encased in a very hard sandstone, however, and were difficult to dig out; they also were incomplete. Most were the remains of sauropods and were much larger and far different from anything found before. Marsh named the first one *Titanosaurus* ("giant lizard"), unaware that that name had already been given to giant dinosaur bones from India. He thought that the complete dinosaur would measure about 50 to 60 feet long from its nose to the tip of its tail.

Cope's disappointment over the Lakes discoveries did not last long. In a location near Cañon City, Colorado, about 80 miles south of where Lakes first found his bones, a school superintendent named O.W. Lucas discovered another fossil bed filled with extremely large dinosaur bones. These bones dated from about the same age as those from Marsh's quarry, but they were in better condition and in softer mudstone and thus easier to dig out. Fortunately for Cope, Lucas contacted him first. Cope acted quickly. He immediately bought the sample bones that Lucas had sent to him and hired a crew to help dig this rich, new site. As summer 1877 drew to a close, Cope had turned the tables on Marsh. Cope announced the discovery of *Camarasaurus*, another long-necked giant, "which exceeds in proportions any other land animal hitherto described, including the one found by Professor Arthur Lakes." This specimen remains one of the most spectacular sauropod skeletons ever discovered.

Marsh soon abandoned the fossil site in Morrison to seek better specimens. In 1877, he received a mysterious letter from Wyoming, signed by two men calling themselves Harlow and Edwards. The letter described a fantastic **bone bed** near Laramie, Wyoming. All these men wanted was some money for their trouble, which Marsh was happy to provide. The two men turned out to be railroad supervisors. They used false names when they first wrote to Marsh in an attempt to guard both their identities and the location of the fossils. Once a deal was struck, they revealed themselves as W.E. Carlin and W.H. Reed.

Marsh sent his best men to the newly discovered fossil site in Wyoming. The bone bed came to be called by the name of the place they were found: Como Bluff. The dinosaur bones were spread across six miles of rocky terrain, and many individual quarries were dug across this expanse. Although not as densely packed with bones as some other, smaller sites, Como Bluff still ranks as one of the most plentiful dinosaur deposits ever discovered. Marsh's team of workers remained at Como Bluff for more than six years. They removed ton after ton of dinosaur bones. By the time they were done, nearly 500 crates of dinosaur bones had been shipped from Como Bluff to New Haven.

Marsh named more than two dozen new dinosaurs from these remains, including some of the most famous dinosaurs of all. Several long-necked dinosaurs were found at Como Bluff, including *"Brontosaurus"* (now known as *Apatosaurus,* or "deceptive lizard"); *Diplodocus* ("double-beam"); *Camarasaurus* ("chamber lizard"); and *Barosaurus* ("heavy lizard"). Perhaps the strangest dinosaur the Marsh team found was *Stegosaurus* ("plated lizard"), the plant eater with a double row of large, triangular plates on its back and spikes on its tail. A large predator was also found at the site, the equally familiar *Allosaurus* ("different lizard").

The great dinosaur bone rush that began with Cope and Marsh in 1877 occupied the two men until their deaths in the 1890s. The fierce competition between Cope and Marsh led to many new dinosaur discoveries but produced many mistakes as well. Of the 149 dinosaur species named by Cope and Marsh, only 37 are accepted by paleontologists today. Many of the species that Cope and Marsh thought were new have proved to be different individuals belonging to the same species. Some of this confusion happened because dinosaur science was so new. These two men were unearthing a parade of strange creatures that had never been seen

*(continues)*

(continued)

before. They were bound to make some mistakes—and science, after all, is an ongoing series of discoveries that improve on previous knowledge. Error—and the correction of error—are vital parts of science. Cope and Marsh opened up a vast, new frontier to the study of dinosaurs. In so doing, they also laid the foundation for future expeditions by other scientists who learned from the mistakes of these two feuding professors.

*(continued from page 73)*

to all forms of sauropods. It appears that sauropods with shorter forelimbs, short dorsal vertebrae, a center of gravity in the area of the pelvis, and strong tails might have been able to do this. The tall brachiosaurs, however, with their long front limbs, probably were unable to achieve this stance as it is sometimes pictured in movies and other dinosaur artwork. For such an animal to get its head aloft in such a way would mean that blood pumped from the heart would have to travel a long distance, against gravity, to get to the brain; there is no known anatomical means of enabling this without the animal's having a heart so large that it would have filled half the body cavity. Thus, even if sauropods could rear up like this, they probably didn't stay aloft for more than a few seconds; otherwise, they would have fainted!

Another factor that contributed to the locomotion of sauropods was the interrelatedness of the mass and strength of their bones and their respiratory system. Interestingly, both of these aspects of dinosaur biology were intimately related through adaptations of sauropod vertebrae. Sauropod limbs were indeed dense and heavy skeletal elements, all the better to support their enormous body masses. Such was not the case with sauropod vertebrae: Throughout the evolution of these enormous animals, there was a trend toward lighter and more pneumatic bones in the spinal column. **Pneumaticity** is the process of filling something with air. In sauropod vertebrae, this meant the evolution of concavities and other hollow spaces in the back bones, giving these bones a highly sculpted appearance, as if they were made of a complex series of thin, bony sheets.

Pneumatic vertebrae affected sauropod locomotion by reducing the weight of the spine without sacrificing strength. The pneumaticity of sauropod bones also represented an enhancement to the dinosaur respiratory system because these animals' bones housed air sacs throughout the body. These air sacs both improved the distribution of oxygen to muscles and tissues and allowed cool air to absorb body heat and be exhaled, thus keeping the animal from overheating. Other than sauropod dinosaurs, only theropods, including birds, are known to have respiratory systems of air sacs located in the thorax and abdomen. In birds, and presumably in non-avian dinosaurs, this respiratory system was unidirectional with respect to the lungs, with air coming into one set of air sacs, then passing through the lungs, and then going out from another set of air sacs through the trachea (windpipe) without passing again through the lungs. This process avoids the pause found in mammal respiration, in which air must be exhaled from the lungs before inhalation can occur again. The pneumatic respiratory system of sauropods, like that of birds, would have been one of the most efficient systems ever to evolve in a terrestrial vertebrate. It allowed sauropods to breathe with great efficiency and keep from overheating, thus improving the animals' ability to support an active lifestyle even with such enormous body mass.

## Sauropod Eggs and Nests

Dinosaurs—like their bird descendants and all known reptiles—hatched from eggs. Dinosaur eggs have been found on every continent but Antarctica and Australia. More than 220 egg sites have been discovered, three-quarters of which are in either North America or Asia. Most of the egg nests that have been found date from the Late Cretaceous Epoch and are from areas that were once relatively dry or semiarid for all or part of the year. Dinosaur egg nests discovered in the Gobi Desert of Mongolia were buried by sudden sandstorms that doomed many dinosaurs along with their unhatched young. Other nesting sites, such as those found in France, India, and northwestern North America, met similar fates in sandstorms, mud slides, and other rapidly occurring natural catastrophes.

Fossil dinosaur eggs come in various shapes and sizes, including round, oval, and elongated oval varieties. The smallest known dinosaur eggs are round and only about 3 inches (7.6 centimeters) in diameter. The largest, found in China, are elongate and about 18 inches (46 centimeters) long.

The largest known dinosaur eggs are not from the sauropods, as one might expect. They are from a theropod group called the therizinosaurs, whose eggs measured up to about 18.5 inches (47 centimeters) long. The producers of these eggs have been positively identified based on a remarkable embryonic skeleton found inside one such egg. The egg containing the embryo was discovered in 1996 in Xixia, China, as part of a nest containing 26 therizinosaur eggs.

The only way to clearly identify the kind of dinosaur that laid an egg is to find a fossilized embryo inside. This is an extremely rare occurrence in the fossil record. The next best guess is based on the kinds of dinosaur bone fragments found in the vicinity of fossil eggs and nests. Another helpful way to identify the producer of a fossil egg is to examine the microscopic structure of the eggshell to see how it compares to the shells of dinosaur eggs that *do* have embryos inside them.

For many years, sauropod dinosaurs have been associated with medium-sized eggs that were roundish in shape. Some of these were spherical and measured about 5 to 10 inches (12.8 to 25.6 centimeters) in diameter. Others were slightly elongated and measured about 9 inches long by 6 inches wide (23 by 15.3 centimeters). Because cases of mistaken identity have previously been made in the study of dinosaur eggs, many scientists have been reluctant to assume that round eggs were laid by sauropods until conclusive evidence was found.

The large, round eggs so often attributed to sauropod dinosaurs have been found in many places around the world, including Spain, France, India, and Argentina. **Clutches** of these eggs generally consist of about 12 closely packed eggs laid in a single layer, although cases with as few as 3 and as many as 20 eggs also have been found. The egg sites in these locations offer our best clues about the nesting habits of sauropods.

Sauropods laid their eggs in three patterns, a habit that was likely governed by the physical size of the mother:

- Six to twelve eggs in a clutch laid in a circular pit that may have been dug out using the large, inside thumb claws on the forelimbs of the adult sauropod. These nest patterns have been found in Spain and Argentina.
- Fifteen to twenty eggs laid in semicircular arcs instead of tight clutches. It appears that this type of pattern, observed in France, may have matched the turning motion of a squatting female as she laid her eggs. The turning motion may have helped her to avoid accidentally stepping on the eggs as they were being deposited.
- Eggs laid in linear pairs or in parallel rows. Found in France, this type of nest is most rare. It is thought to have been made by sauropods due to the shape and size of the eggs.

Sauropod nesting grounds sometimes contain nests that have been stacked on top of other nests. This evidence suggests a seasonal return of the dinosaurs to the same nesting grounds, where they created new nests on top of the remains of old ones.

### Sauropod Embryos and Nesting Grounds

The first indisputable evidence that sauropods laid round eggs came in late 1998 from the desolate badlands of Argentina known as Patagonia. A small expedition from the American Museum of Natural History was exploring a remote corner of northwestern Patagonia for evidence of fossil birds. The team was led by Luis Chiappe, an Argentine himself, and Lowell Dingus, both then of the American Museum of Natural History in New York. Joining them from Argentina was Rodolfo Coria (b. 1961) of the Carmen Funes Museum in Plaza Huincul. Coria is a skilled and conscientious paleontologist who has found himself in the middle of an extraordinary period of dinosaur discoveries in his native land. He led the teams that discovered and named *Argentinosaurus* and *Giganotosaurus,* among the largest known sauropod and theropod dinosaurs, respectively. His base of operation is a humble little museum that has barely enough space to house these important discoveries. Scientists from around the world have begun to visit Coria's home turf, working alongside him and his team on many joint projects.

Rudolfo Coria is a skilled and conscientious paleontologist who finds himself in the middle of an extraordinary period of dinosaur discoveries in his native land. He led the teams that found and named *Argentinosaurus* and *Giganotosaurus,* two of the largest known dinosaurs. His base of operation is a small museum with barely enough space to house these important discoveries. Scientists from around the world have begun to visit Coria on his home turf to work alongside him and his team on many joint projects.

During its second day in the field, the American Museum of Natural History expedition spotted a promising rock face in the distance that might contain fossils. Having driven as far as they could in their truck, the paleontologists stopped and began to walk in the direction of the rock face. Before too long, they noticed fossil fragments all around them on the ground. Step by step, the team members all began to find fossilized chunks of dinosaur eggs. "We realized that the entire place was virtually paved with these eggs and fragments of eggs," recalled Chiappe. "The concentration of eggs was so intense and rich that, in an area of roughly 100 yards by 200 yards, we counted about 195 clusters of eggs."

Each cluster of eggs contained a half-dozen or more eggs. Each egg was only about five or six inches (12 to 15 cm) in diameter and nearly round. The outside surface of the fossil egg fragments had a familiar pitted pattern that had been seen before in dinosaur eggs. The scientists soon realized that they were walking through a vast nesting site of some kind of dinosaur. Dinosaur eggs are one of the rarest fossil discoveries, yet here they were surrounded by thousands of them. It was the discovery of a lifetime.

The team immediately set to work collecting fossils. During the first short season, they recovered several excellent egg specimens and returned to the United States to examine them in a laboratory. In early 1998, Marilyn Fox, an expert at reconstructing fossil specimens, was carefully chipping rock out from inside one of the fossils when she discovered something extraordinary—tiny bones. The egg contained the fossilized remains of an unhatched dinosaur embryo. After weeks of slow and painstaking preparation with the most delicate of hand tools, the dinosaur embryo began to reveal its identity. It became clear that the tiny dinosaur embryo belonged to the clade that includes some of the largest dinosaurs—the titanosaurs. These members of the group were probably between 40 and 60 feet (12 and 18 meters) when fully grown.

To the delight of the scientists, many of the intact eggs and fragments contained fossilized pieces of embryonic titanosaurs. The team even recovered fossil skin casts—impressions of dinosaur skin—the first for any variety of embryonic dinosaur specimen. The skin pattern clearly showed the reptilian scales that made up the skin of the embryo. Had they lived, these embryonic titanosaurs that measured about 12 inches (30 cm) long inside the egg would one day have grown to be 60 feet (18 m) long.

The discoverers named the site Auca Mahuevo. The name combined a reference to an extinct volcano in the area named Auca Mahuida with the Spanish words *más huevos*, meaning "more eggs." The expedition team returned to the site for three more years.

The size and scale of the Patagonian egg site are so extensive that Coria believes the site will take many years to explore fully. He calls the site "unique," a once-in-a-lifetime opportunity to study the entire ecosystem of these dinosaurs. The area includes fossils not only of the titanosaurs and their eggs, but also of ancient plant life and other creatures, including other dinosaurs, that lived in the same area with the titanosaurs.

The titanosaur embryos from Patagonia join only a small group of embryonic remains known for any dinosaurs. There are just four other examples of embryonic dinosaur skeletons that have been positively associated with dinosaur eggs, and only one of these skeletons represents a species of sauropod.

Though quite rare, probable sauropod eggs have been found in many countries around the world. The first fossil egg fragments thought to be those of dinosaurs were of this kind. They were found in the Provence region of France and described by Jean-Jacque Pouech in 1859. Since then, eggs associated with sauropods, especially titanosaurs, have been found in India, Argentina, Spain, and Mongolia. Thus far, however, no sauropod eggs are known from the Jurassic Period.

## SUMMARY

This chapter investigated the traits, lifestyles, and members of the sauropods that thrived during the Middle and Late Jurassic, the heyday of the largest herbivorous dinosaurs.

1. Sauropods were the tallest, heaviest, and longest animals to ever walk the Earth. They were members of the saurischian clade known as Sauropodomorpha, which also included the "Prosauropoda." "Prosauropods" and sauropods shared a common ancestor.

2. The earliest known sauropod is *Antetonitrus* (Late Triassic, South Africa), dating from 220 million to 215 million years ago.

3. The anatomical features of sauropods that made them a unique clade of dinosaurs revolved around two aspects of their lifestyle—a tendency toward gigantism and their vegetarian diet.

4. General anatomical features shared by all sauropods included long necks and tails, straight and strong limbs, four or more sacral vertebrae, and small skulls optimized for stripping leaves from plants.

5. Sauropods are divided into two main groups: Eusauropoda, somewhat primitive members from the Early to Late

Jurassic; and Neosauropoda, from the Middle Jurassic to Late Cretaceous.

6. Sauropods were medium- to high-browsing herbivores. Their teeth were able to pluck and strip leaves from trees. Digestion was aided by stomach stones for grinding plant material.

7. Metabolism is the combination of all biochemical processes that take place in an organism to keep it alive.

8. Thermoregulation in dinosaurs ranged from probable endothermy in birds and the theropods most closely related to them to homeothermy in sauropods and other gigantic species.

9. Homeothermy allowed sauropods and other kinds of large dinosaurs to maintain high body temperatures while still having lower, "cold-blooded" metabolic rates.

10. Mobility in sauropods was aided by sturdy limbs, having a center of gravity near the pelvic region, and the lightness of their vertebral column due to the pneumaticity of the vertebrae.

11. Sauropods laid moderately large, round eggs in circular pits, semicircular arcs, and parallel rows, a factor seemingly governed by the size of the mother.

# THEROPOD DIVERSITY: GIANT PREDATORY DINOSAURS

Theropods—the clade of carnivorous dinosaurs (and a number of later taxa that converted to herbivory)—first appeared in the Late Triassic. Their origins and early diversification are recounted in *Dawn of the Dinosaur Age*. Like sauropods, theropods were saurischians, with a unique dinosaurian hip structure that encouraged mobility and the evolution of large body sizes. This is not to say that all theropods were giants, or that all giant dinosaurs were saurischians, however; the theropods also included some of the smallest known non-avian dinosaurs, as well as birds.

As with sauropods, the Middle and Late Jurassic were a time of increased diversity in theropod evolution. As sauropods grew to larger and larger sizes, dominating the world of herbivorous vertebrates, so, too, did theropods become increasingly specialized in their carnivorous adaptations, size, range, and weaponry. Although the largest of the theropods are generally associated with the Cretaceous Period, some theropods approaching the size of tyrannosaurs began to appear during the Late Jurassic. These included some supersized specimens of *Allosaurus* (Late Jurassic, western United States) and *Sinraptor* (Middle Jurassic, China), two enormous predators capable of attacking the largest plant-eating dinosaurs. At the other end of scale of theropod size, an equally important evolutionary trend took place in the Middle to Late Jurassic: adaptations in small theropods leading to the evolution of feathers and flight.

This chapter describes the continuing evolution of predatory dinosaurs during the Middle and Late Jurassic Epochs and adaptations that led to their continued success.

## EVOLUTION OF THE THEROPODS

Recent cladistic analyses of theropods by leading paleontologists—including Jacques Gauthier (Yale University); Paul Sereno (University of Chicago); Thomas Holtz Jr. (University of Maryland); and Michael Benton (University of Bristol)—do not agree entirely on the placements of many genera but have led to some general agreement regarding the higher level of classification of these dinosaurs. Theropods may be defined as all of the descendants of the common ancestor of both *Coelophysis* (Late Triassic, New Mexico) and Aves (birds). Accordingly, the following categories are used here and in other books in the series *The Prehistoric Earth* to organize the discussion of theropods.

The categories used to organize the discussion of theropods are depicted in the figure Dinosaur Clades and Relationships: **Theropoda**.

*Ceratosauria* (Late Triassic to Late Cretaceous Epochs). These are the most primitive theropods. This group includes theropods more closely related to *Ceratosaurus* than to birds. This clade includes *Coelophysis*, *Dilophosaurus*, *Ceratosaurus*, and others.

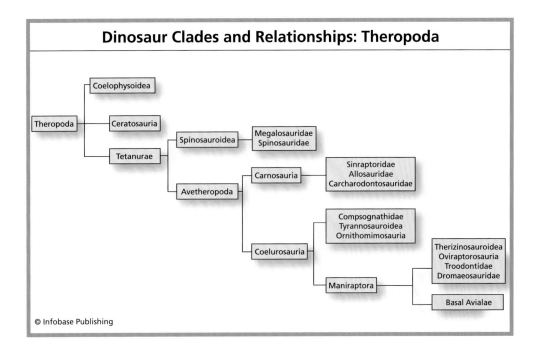

**Dinosaur Clades and Relationships: Theropoda**

© Infobase Publishing

*Tetanurae* (Early Jurassic to Late Cretaceous Epochs). These are the most derived, nonceratosaurian theropods. Tetanurans are defined as modern birds and any theropods that share a more recent common ancestor with birds than with *Ceratosaurus*. The category of Tetanurae is further divided into two major subgroups. The most primitive, least derived, basal tetanurans are in the subgroup **Spinosauroidea**. The more derived tetanurans are in the subgroup **Avetheropoda**.

Among the Spinosauroidea were the largest of all theropods—the spinosaurs, from North Africa. The Avetheropoda made up the largest theropod group and included many well-known genera that populated the Northern and Southern Hemispheres during the Jurassic and Cretaceous Periods. These included giants such as *Tyrannosaurus*, *Giganotosaurus*, and *Carcharodontosaurus;* ostrich-like dinosaurs; the sickle-clawed dromaeosaurs popularly known as "raptors"; and others, including various taxa of feathered dinosaurs that led to modern birds.

This book, *Time of the Giants*, will explore some members of the first and second of these groups, the Ceratosauria and earlier, more basal members of the Tetanurae.

## Ceratosauria

Members of the Ceratosauria represent the earliest substantial radiation of carnivorous dinosaurs. The earliest ceratosaurs lived during the Late Triassic and Early Jurassic. Several other prominent lines of ceratosaurs persisted, particularly in regions of the Southern Hemisphere (now Argentina, India, and Madagascar) well into the Late Cretaceous Epoch. The name *Ceratosauria* is a nod to *Ceratosaurus* (Late Jurassic, Colorado and Utah), a predatory dinosaur with a small horn on its snout, named in 1884 by American paleontologist Othniel Charles Marsh. With the exception of the Gondwanan Cretaceous taxa, ceratosaurs were largely extinct by the Middle Jurassic. Among the ceratosaurs that lived among the giants of the Late Jurassic were two curious holdovers from the early evolution of theropods, *Ceratosaurus* and *Elaphrosaurus*.

*Ceratosaurus* was a medium- to large-sized predator, the original specimen of which measured about 20 feet (6.1 m) long. Very fragmentary remains of other *Ceratosaurus*-like dinosaurs have been found in such places as Portugal and Tanzania; the Tanzania specimen suggests a dinosaur that may have been more than 40 feet (12 m) long.

The skull of *Ceratosaurus* was tall and broad, with a wide snout, strong jaws, and large, bladelike teeth. Its head was adorned with a single stout horn on top of the skull in front of the eyes, as well as smaller hornlets over the eyes. It has been suggested that *Ceratosaurus,* with a tail shaped somewhat like that of a crocodile, may have preferred hunting in the water for aquatic prey. The *Ceratosaurus* body plan included a short, stocky neck, long hind limbs, a stout tail and strong but short forelimbs.

Marsh's original specimens, discovered in the 1880s, accounted for most of what was known of this theropod until the recent discovery, in the years since 1999, of new specimens, including a juvenile. One study of the **braincase** of a new specimen included work done by radiologist R. Kent Sanders and paleontologist David K. Smith using computed tomography, or CT scans. Although the brains of fossil animals are never preserved, the endocranial cavity in which the brain was located can sometimes reveal much about the sensory abilities of a given dinosaur. A scientist familiar with the physiology of the vertebrate brain can trace channels and spaces within a braincase that once hosted connections to nerves and sensory mechanisms of the brain and body. In the case of *Ceratosaurus*, the position of the brain and associated nerve canals confirms a posture for the head and neck that was more horizontal than erect, eyesight that was probably about average, and a well-formed sense of smell comparable to that of birds.

*Elaphrosaurus* is a less well understood ceratosaur from the Late Jurassic of Tanzania. The original specimen, described in 1920, lacked a head and most of the forelimb. Measuring about 17 feet (5 m) long, *Elaphrosaurus* had a slender body and a long neck and was undoubtedly a more agile runner than the bulkier *Ceratosaurus*.

The lightweight body of *Elaphrosaurus* once led paleontologists to classify it as an ostrichlike dinosaur; but more recent cladistic analysis has demonstrated that its feet, vertebrae, pelvis, and leg bones were more closely aligned with those of ceratosaurs.

## Tetanurae

The group known as tetanurans includes theropods that share a more recent common ancestor with birds than with *Ceratosaurus*. This means that these theropods were more advanced in their anatomical adaptations than the primitive Ceratosauria. The majority of theropods belong to the group Tetanurae. The name Tetanurae means "stiff tails" and refers to the fact that the ends of the tails of these theropods were stiffened by interlocking connections on the vertebrae. Many of the most famous tetanurans lived during the Cretaceous Period, but a number of less derived, more basal members of the group lived during the Middle and Late Jurassic and are known as basal tetanurans. The basal tetanurans exhibit important trends in the evolution of meat-eating dinosaurs and are represented by spectacular predators such as *Allosaurus* (Late Jurassic, western United States) and also by tiny meat-eaters, including *Compsognathus* (Late Jurassic, Germany and France).

Tetanurans were more like birds than were members of the Ceratosauria and were the stock from which modern birds arose. Other anatomical features shared by most tetanurans included at least one small, accessory opening in between the antorbital fenestra and the nostril opening, further lightening the skull); a muscular ridge on the shoulder blade; the positioning of all of the teeth in front of the eye; the absence of fanglike teeth in the lower jaw; and modifications to the bones of the hands, the upper leg bone, and the knee joints. Basal tetanurans possessed all of these traits but in a less developed or derived form than later tetanurans.

Early tetanurans that lived during the Middle and Late Jurassic are divided in the two major divisions and associated theropod subgroups, the Spinosauroidea and the Avetheropoda.

*Megalosaurus* jaw

### *Spinosauroidea*

Spinosauroidea is a group of medium- to large-bodied theropods that itself is divided into two subgroups, the Megalosauridae and Spinosauridae.

*Megalosauridae.* This clade is represented by six genera known from largely incomplete remains. The name of the clade is derived from *Megalosaurus* (Middle Jurassic, England), or "great lizard"—a poorly known yet famous theropod because of its prominent place in the history of dinosaur science. The first specimen was discovered in a slab of slate in England in the early 1820s. The specimen included only the right half of the lower jaw and teeth. It became the first dinosaur to be described scientifically when professor William Buckland (1784–1856) named and wrote about it in 1824. Still poorly known, the genus *Megalosaurus* was for many years a convenient category for categorizing other poorly known large theropods—fragmentary, medium-sized theropods that lacked enough material to adequately classify them were often just referred to "*Megalosaurus*" or as pertaining to "a megalosaur." Other taxa grouped with the Jurassic megalosaurs are somewhat better known but far from complete, including *Torvosaurus* (Late Jurassic, Utah, Colorado, and Wyoming) and *Eustreptospondylus* (Middle Jurassic, England).

*Spinosauridae.* Six genera that belong in this clade are currently known. Spinosaurs—including *Baryonyx* (Early Cretaceous, England and Spain); *Suchomimus* (Early Cretaceous, Niger); *Irritator* (Early Cretaceous, Brazil); and *Spinosaurus* (Late Cretaceous, Egypt and Morocco)—were among the largest predatory dinosaurs of the Cretaceous Period. Traits included a long, very narrow snout; a narrow skull; a long neck and long arms; and a ridge along the back that was sometimes highly pronounced and sail-like. Spinosaurs are generally interpreted as fish eaters. They are discussed in greater detail in *Last of the Dinosaurs*.

### Avetheropoda

The clade known as the Avetheropoda includes some of the most remarkably complete remains of theropods. Curiously, it includes the largest theropods in one group, the Carnosauria, and the smallest predatory dinosaurs in a second group, the Coelurosauria. The name Avetheropod—"bird theropods" or "bird-beast foot"—refers to the birdlike feet of these predators. Traits uniting avetheropods include an extra fenestra in the upper jaw area and changes the roof of the mouth and back of the skull, as well as modifications to limbs and increased stiffening of the tail.

**Carnosauria**. All known members of this clade are large bodied. Only 5 of the 13 members of this clade date from the Middle to Late Jurassic. The best known carnosaur is *Allosaurus* (Late Jurassic, western United States), a large theropod known from several complete skulls and skeletons from more than 60 specimens collected since its discovery in 1877 by a fossil-collecting team working for Othniel Charles Marsh. At the time of its discovery, *Allosaurus* ("other lizard") was the largest known predatory dinosaur. Curiously, Marsh's archrival Edward Drinker Cope had found a more complete specimen of the same dinosaur prior to Marsh but had not had time to examine it before Marsh found, and named, his own specimen.

Although similar in basic body form to later theropods such as *Tyrannosaurus*, the carnosaurs actually were a separate line of theropods that were less closely related to birds than is *Tyrannosaurus*. Weighing up to three tons and measuring about 40 feet (12 m) long, *Allosaurus* was the most common large (and probably the top) predator of the Late Jurassic American West. It was one of the only predators capable of bringing down a large sauropod, although one might speculate that its most common prey victims were likely younger, smaller individuals or species that could pose less of a threat of attack. The skull of *Allosaurus* was adorned with prominent hornlets over the eyes, and its powerful jaws were lined with moderately large, bladelike teeth for slicing its prey.

Paleontologist Emily Rayfield of Cambridge University recently studied the bite and stress forces that probably took place in the skull of *Allosaurus*. Using noninvasive computed tomography (CT) scans to investigate the allosaur skull, Rayfield determined that the power of the bite was focused at the front of the jaw, resulting in a "slash and tear" approach to feeding that reduced stress on the teeth. Using this technique, an allosaur would grip its prey with its front teeth and swing its head from side to side to rip off meat.

Among the other known Jurassic carnosaurs are four genera from various parts of the world: *Lourinhanosaurus* (Late Jurassic, Portugal); *Monolophosaurus* (Middle Jurassic, China); *Sinraptor* (Middle Jurassic, China); and *Yangchuanosaurus* (Late Jurassic, China). *Sinraptor* ("China thief") is the best known of these and is represented by a nearly complete skull and skeleton first described in 1993 by a joint Canadian-Chinese paleontological team headed by Phil Currie (Royal Tyrrell Museum) and Dong Zhiming (Institute of Vertebrate Paleontology and Paleoanthropology). *Sinraptor* was a slender predator that measured about 25 feet (7.5 m) long.

The Carnosauria survived into the Cretaceous Period, with several famous, very-large-bodied carnosaur predators evolving during this time, including members of the Carcharodontosauridae, such as *Carcharodontosaurus* (Early Cretaceous, Egypt, Algeria, and Niger) and *Giganotosaurus* and *Mapusaurus* (Early Cretaceous, Argentina), both of which are described in more detail in *Last of the Dinosaurs*.

*Coelurosauria.* Most coelurosaurs were relatively small, although a few attained sizes that rivaled the giant spinosaurids and carcharodontosaurs. It is within this group that birds reside. Anatomical traits uniting the coelurosaurs included forelimbs that were more than half as long as the hind limbs, long second and third digits on the hand, enlargement of the fenestrae in front of the eye socket, and modifications of the hind foot that improved speed and agility.

While most coelurosaurs date from the Cretaceous Period, *Compsognathus* was a basal coelurosaurian from the Late Jurassic of Germany and France. About the size of a chicken, this small, lightweight predator is known from excellent specimens found in fine-grained limestone. What these fossils reveal is a delicate creature that was extraordinarily birdlike but lacked wings.

Several groups of coelurosaurs evolved during the Cretaceous, including the gigantic tyrannosaurs and smaller oviraptorosaurs and the dromaeosaurs, which are detailed in *Last of the Dinosaurs*. The relationship of *Compsognathus* to later coelurosaurs is uncertain.

## PREDATORY LIVES

The evolution of predatory adaptations in vertebrates reached an awesome yet elegant apex in the anatomy and behavior of carnivorous dinosaurs. One should not dwell too long on the fate of the dinosaurs that fell prey to these creatures, however, because the prey animals also extended the size, specializations, and population numbers of their kind to similarly impressive levels. The existence of large predators such as *Allosaurus* and the later tyrannosaurs, spinosaurs, and carcharodontosaurs is evidence that prey animals such as iguanodonts, hadrosaurs, sauropods, and horned dinosaurs existed in great numbers and so successfully occupied their

respective niches in the world of browsing vegetarians that predatory dinosaurs had to adapt highly specialized weapons and techniques to hunt them down.

The predatory lifestyle of theropods is reflected in many aspects
of their anatomy. Clues in the bones of theropods allow paleontologists to reflect on the likely behaviors and lifestyles of these animals
as living organisms.

## Senses

Predatory creatures rely on their senses to find their next meal.
The **olfactory** organs enable a predator to detect the smell of a prey
animal or carcass long before it is in sight. The **otic**, or auditory,
function alerts a predator to the spatial proximity of a prey animal
before it can be seen. A keen **optic** function—excellent vision—is
important to pinpoint and run down the prey once it has been
located. All of these senses were certainly important to predatory
dinosaurs, and their skulls sometimes contain clues as to the acuity
of these senses.

The brains of modern vertebrates—and particularly the brains of
reptiles and birds—are similar in many ways. The braincase in the
skull, including the brain cavity, holds the brain and the many con-
necting nerve bundles that connect the brain to other parts of the
body. Nerves connect the brain to other organs through holes in the
braincase. Dinosaur skulls show many of the same kinds of connections found in modern vertebrates. The sense of smell was located at
the front of the brain, in the olfactory lobe, and vision was concen-
trated in an optic lobe near its center. Study of the fossil braincases
of various theropods confirms that their senses were moderately to
highly acute, as one would expect for specialized predators.

*Vision.* The eyes of theropods were larger than those in other
kinds of dinosaurs of similar size. The eyes were especially large in
the smaller, later, big-brained theropods such as *Troodon*.

While most theropods had eyes that could look only to the
sides, like those of a horse or a lizard, many of the later theropods,
including *Tyrannosaurus*, had eyes that were more forward-looking,

providing **binocular vision** in which the areas that each eye sees overlap with each another. Binocular vision allows an animal to more accurately track and pinpoint objects—such as moving prey—in its field of vision, thus making it easier to focus on a prey animal that moves in an evasive manner.

In a recent study of theropod skulls, paleontologist Kent Stevens analyzed the binocular field of vision of seven theropod dinosaurs. He found that the eyesight of less advanced theropods, including the basal tetanurans *Allosaurus* and *Carcharodontosaurus*, was not as binocular as that of more advanced and later theropods such as *Tyrannosaurus*, *Troodon*, and *Velociraptor*. The tyrannosaurs had particularly excellent binocular vision, equaling and possibly exceeding that of the modern hawk, a bird known for its impressive vision.

*Hearing.* The acuity of theropod hearing can be determined by examining the brain cavity as well as the parts of the skull that may have contained hearing bones.

Some theropods appear to have had special adaptations for hearing. *Troodon* and some other small- to medium-sized coelurosaurian predators had large, complicated inner ears that probably helped them detect the source of a sound more accurately. These adaptations also may have allowed the animals to detect low-frequency sounds more readily, such as the distant footfall of a large plant eater or even the low bellow of a duck-billed dinosaur communicating with its herd.

*Smell.* In its arsenal of sensory weapons, a theropod's sense of smell may have ranked up with its eyesight and good hearing.

The olfactory potential of tyrannosaurs has been studied closely by Christopher Brochu of the Field Museum of Natural History. Brochu has done extensive computed tomography (CT) work on the skull of "Sue," one of the most complete *Tyrannosaurus* skeletons ever found. It was nicknamed after Sue Hendrickson, the field paleontologist who found it. Brochu fabricated a digital endocast of the brain and olfactory bulbs of Sue. The olfactory bulbs of this specimen were proportionately larger than those seen in other examples of theropod skulls, suggesting that these giant coelurosaurian theropods had achieved remarkable senses of smell. The hole in the braincase through which these nerves passed was about the diameter of a peach. By comparison, a smaller hole in the back of the braincase, where the brain connected to the spinal cord, is closer to the size of a grape. Both *Allosaurus* and *Ceratosaurus*, from the Jurassic, have been shown to have relatively large olfactory bulbs and therefore good senses of smell, though perhaps not as good as tyrannosaurs

## Theropod Speed

The speeds at which theropods could run has been a source of speculation and debate for many years. As they consider the question of potential speeds, paleontologists draw on fossil trackways for direct evidence of dinosaur locomotion, on an understanding of dinosaur limb anatomy, and on assumptions regarding metabolism and potential energy expenditure as compared to the physiology of extant animals.

Fossil footprints, and especially trackways, left behind by dinosaurs are the best evidence about the locomotory behavior of dinosaurs.

It is usually not possible to identify the maker of such tracks; but tracks made by theropod dinosaurs, with their three bird-like talons, are easily distinguishable from those of herbivorous dinosaurs. Most trackways are not long and almost always show an animal walking rather than running; this makes sense because running through soft sediment, a surface that is good for capturing footprints, puts an animal in danger of slipping and falling much more than does running on hard ground. There is, however, some trackway evidence for running theropods that has been studied to determine speed.

It is also worth noting, however, that it is impossible to associate a particular set of footprints with any species of dinosaur unless the tracks lead directly to the body of the track-making animal. (This has never yet happened with a dinosaur.) Also, determining the leg length involves either unproveable guesswork as to which animal made the tracks or using some statistics to find generalizations about the group of track-making animals. For theropods, hip height is generally perceived as somewhere between four and five times the length of the footprint. Of course, there always are the possibilities of exceptions: Among birds, for example, jacanas have huge feet for their relatively short legs, so hip height and footprint length do not fall into the same range. Still, this sort of generalization from statistics is the best technique presently available.

To calculate dinosaur speed from trackways, paleontologists use a formula that takes into consideration the length of the stride and the length of a dinosaur's leg from the ground to the hip. Zoologist R. McNeill Alexander is an expert on the biomechanics of animals. In 1976, he first worked out a formula to calculate speed from trackways that is widely used today. Alexander applied his formula to several kinds of theropod trackways. The top theropod speed he calculated from the trackways of a small theropod, probably of the ostrich-dinosaur variety, was 27 mph (16.8 km/hr). This is faster than a human can run, somewhat slower than a racehorse, and about the same speed as a galloping antelope. How long a theropod could maintain such speed is, however, unknown.

Trackways for large running theropods are scarce, and none have been found for a creature the size of *Tyrannosaurus*. Educated guesses are all that can be made about the speed of the largest theropods. In the 1980s, paleontologists Gregory Paul and Robert Bakker proposed that tyrannosaurs and ornithomimosaurs ("ostrich-mimic dinosaurs") were fast runners, with top speeds ranging from 30 to 45 mph (18.7 to 28 km/hr). Several anatomical features of those dinosaurs led Paul and Bakker to that conclusion. These features included the long limbs, powerful thigh and calf muscles, shock-absorbing and flexible knees and ankles, and long, narrow, three-toed feet shared by such theropods.

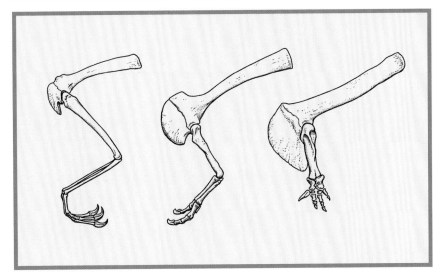

Variation in theropod forelimbs (from left): *Struthiomimus, Tyrannosaurus, Carnotaurus* (not to scale)

Most other paleontologists are not as convinced about fast-running theropods, however. Much of this lack of conviction is due to uncertainty over the metabolic rate of the large theropods. Most paleontologists think that a top speed for *Tyrannosaurus* of 45 mph was unlikely except, perhaps, for a very short period of time. Paleontologist James O. Farlow went a step further by suggesting that a large theropod risked serious injury if it fell while running at high speed. Farlow questioned whether it made sense for such animals ever to do so.

The recent work of mechanical engineer John Hutchinson of Stanford University has also dampened enthusiasm for fast-running giant theropods. Using a computer model to simulate the anatomy of a running *T. rex*, Hutchinson and his colleagues calculated how much leg muscle a terrestrial animal would require to support running at various speeds. "As animals get really enormous," explained Hutchinson, "eventually to support their weight

*(continues on page 102)*

# THINK ABOUT IT

## Dinosaur Intelligence

Is it possible to determine the intelligence of dinosaurs? If intelligence is defined as the ability to reason and learn, it would seem impossible to know this about dinosaurs without having the opportunity to observe them in life. Surprisingly, paleontologists are not entirely without some clues about the intelligence of extinct animals—clues based on evidence from the fossil record. Chief among these is the relative size of the dinosaur brain, with *relative* meaning "compared to the size of the body the brain controlled."

The size of an animal does not determine how intelligent it is. A bigger animal is not necessarily a smarter one. Similarly, the size of the brain does not determine how intelligent an animal is, and a bigger brain is not necessarily a smarter one. What is more important is the weight of the brain in proportion to the weight of the body. By this measure, people have a large brain in proportion to a relatively small body size. Birds and mammals score higher than reptiles, amphibians, and fish when it comes to brain-weight-to-body-weight ratios. This places mammals at the top of the "intelligence" pyramid in today's animal kingdom, a conclusion that most people can agree with if one loosely defines intelligence as the ability to reason and learn.

The brain, like other soft tissues and organs, does not fossilize. The approximate size of a dinosaur's brain can be determined either by casting, or by computed tomography (CT) scanning, and then measuring the cavity inside the skull that once held the brain. Having a dinosaur skull, however, does not guarantee that the brain cavity inside the skull is preserved well enough to measure. Most dinosaur skull material is fragmentary, often missing part or all of the braincase bones that surround the cavity. Even when a complete braincase is present, skulls are often distorted due to compression and crushing of the bones during fossilization, thus making measurements of the braincase less accurate. The advent of CT scanning during the past 10 years has provided a noninvasive way for paleontologists to measure the braincase inside a skull. As a result, knowledge about dinosaur brains is slowly expanding for those dinosaurs represented by good skull material. Even so, measurements of dinosaur braincases have thus far been made for less than 5 percent of all known taxa.

The size of the brain alone is not a measure of intelligence. When studies of brain size are combined with studies of living animals, however, scientists can establish a rough link between the weight of the brain, the weight of the body, and observable intelligence. In the largest kinds of living animals, such as the elephant, the ratio of brain weight to body weight is predictably lower than that seen in smaller animals—such as a dog or cat—even though a high level of intelligence is still present. This means that the brain itself does not have to be huge in a huge animal for the animal to be smart. Overall body size is an important consideration when dealing with dinosaurs because of their tendency toward gigantism.

In the world of dinosaur brain sizes, theropods generally had a higher brain-weight-to-body-weight ratio. Small theropods, such as *Troodon*, had the largest known brains in comparison to body weight. This made them comparable to some modern birds and mammals. Many other dinosaurs, although maybe not as gifted, were still comparable to modern crocodylians and other reptiles when it came to the sizes of their brains compared to body weight.

In considering the intelligence of dinosaurs it is also instructive to keep in mind that the parts of the brain come in many different sizes, and that not all parts of the brain are (or even could be) involved in reasoning. Many dinosaurs had highly developed parts of their brains that were involved instead in smell, sight, and other senses. It is also important to keep in mind that intelligence itself is not the be-all and end-all of things, and that the longevity of a species does not depend on intelligence. That is, the ability to reason is by no means a requirement for an animal to function or survive; the animal only has to have enough brain function

*(continues)*

*(continued)*

to enable it to function in its ecological niche. Humans are by no means "better" than other animals because they have bigger brains. Humans are better at reasoning and abstract thought but are not better at, for example, doing what elephants do, or what voles or owls do. The brains of those creatures are adapted for doing what they do. It is not a matter of "better" or "worse."

*(continued from page 99)*

their muscles have to be bigger and bigger and bigger. But as they get bigger, they add more mass." Eventually, the large size of an animal prevents it from adding more muscle to support its growing weight, and a ratio between muscle mass and body weight is achieved. Hutchinson concluded that a biomechanically reasonable speed range for *Tyrannosaurus* was between 10 and 25 mph (6 to 16 km/hr). It is important to note that Hutchinson's conclusions were based strictly on mechanical aspects of tyrannosaur anatomy and did not take into consideration the possible metabolic rate of giant theropods.

## Killing Tactics

Insights about the possible hunting and killing methods of theropods spring from a variety of studies. Some paleontologists, including Emily Rayfield and Greg Erickson, have studied the bite and stress forces of theropods using computed tomography and scale models to understand the skull mechanics of biting. Others, including theropod expert Thomas Holtz, have drawn on an understanding of the whole animal, synthesizing anatomical knowledge about theropod jaws, teeth, sensory acuity, locomotion, and weaponry with observations of extant predators. Holtz has suggested three categories of killing strategies that may have been used by theropods.

*Grapple-and-slash predators.* These predators usually wait in hiding to ambush their prey and then use their forelimbs to seize prey after a very short chase. They kill their prey with a combination of grappling claws on the forelimb, bites, and bruising kicks from the hind limbs. Prey may be suffocated by a bite that covers the nose or that holds the prey's mouth shut, or the predator may clamp down on the throat and crush the trachea (windpipe). Among extant carnivores, large cats such as tigers and cheetahs are grapple-and-slash predators.

Dromaeosaurs used an even more specialized version of the grapple-and-slash technique. Equipped with a large "sickle" claw on the second toe of each foot, dromaeosaurs had proportionately shorter legs than other theropods, so it is likely that dromaeosaurs did not chase their prey for long. Their long arms and hands—with three long, clawed fingers and a flexible wrist—gave them the ability to grasp a prey animal firmly. The toe claw retracted up out of the way when the animal walked but could be flipped down, like an open switchblade knife, when the dromaeosaur was on the attack. Such an arsenal leaves little to the imagination.

One of the larger dromaeosaurs was *Deinonychus*, named "terrible claw" after its formidable foot claw. Everything about its anatomy suggests that this dromaeosaur was an energetic, swift-running animal. After closing in on its prey, *Deinonychus* probably launched its attack by leaping at the victim feet first, with toe claws extended, gaining a foothold on the prey, and puncturing it with its claws. Thus would the bloodbath begin; the prey, weakened considerably, soon would be unable to struggle. Using its forelimbs to hold the prey, *Deinonychus* could finish it off by biting and continuing to inflict puncture wounds with its feet. One spectacular fossil from Mongolia provides proof of such grapple-and-slash behavior: A *Velociraptor* (Late Cretaceous, Mongolia) is clasped in a death grip with the herbivorous *Protoceratops* (Late Cretaceous, Mongolia), an early horned dinosaur. The theropod is positioned in the way that paleontologists would expect to find in a grapple-and-slash attacker, with its feet kicking the underbelly of the small prey.

*Grapple-and-bite predators.* These predators are also ambushers and use their claws to hold the prey while the jaws do the killing. Hawks, eagles, and other modern birds of prey (which are correctly called "raptors") use this technique. Large theropods other than the short-armed *Tyrannosaurus* were probably of the grapple-and-bite variety. These large theropods included such giants as *Allosaurus*, *Spinosaurus*, *Giganotosaurus*, and *Carcharodontosaurus*. The claws were used to bring down the prey, but the primary killing weapon was the teeth. Unlike the bananalike teeth of tyrannosaurs, the teeth in these other predators were narrow and bladelike. They were excellent for slicing chunks of flesh from their victims.

*Pursuit-and-bite predators.* This type of predator brings down its prey with its jaws after a fairly long chase and then completes the kill using a combination of biting and suffocation. Modern wolves, other dogs, and hyenas use this technique. The claws are mostly used to hold down the prey animal rather than to slash it. Tyrannosaurs probably used this method, taking advantage of their long legs, huge raptorial feet, muscular necks, and jaws lined with sturdy, bone-crunching teeth. Tyrannosaurs probably fed by clamping down on the body of the prey with their jaws, then pulling and twisting with their enormous strength to severely damage bones, muscles, and internal organs and, if possible, rip chunks of meat and bone from the prey.

No matter which technique the predator used, attacking a large herbivore had its risks. If the herbivore was protected with weaponry, such as horns or a sturdy tail club, the theropod might risk its life by challenging a healthy adult. The huge weight and strength of the largest sauropods and hadrosaurs could be used to deflect or injure a pursuing predator. Although theropods were surefooted, their anatomy did not allow them to step to the side; this made them vulnerable to the sideways swipe of a plant eater's heavy tail. These tails may have weighed between 1,000 and 3,000 pounds (450 and 1,360 kg), depending on the kind of plant eater. A blow from such a tail could knock even the largest theropod over, perhaps injuring it severely, while the plant eater made its getaway. For this reason, it is safe to assume that predatory dinosaurs, like most living predators, may often have chosen young or infirm individuals as prey.

## *ARCHAEOPTERYX*: THE FIRST BIRD

The pantheon of Late Jurassic theropods is also distinguished by the appearance of the oldest known bird. One fossil of *Archaeopteryx* ("ancient wing")—from the Late Jurassic-age limestone deposits of Solnhofen, Germany, and known as the Berlin specimen because it resides in a museum in Berlin, Germany—has been called the most valuable fossil ever found. Described in 1861 by German paleontologist Hermann von Meyer (1801–1869), *Archaeopteryx* is the earliest known bird and represents something of a transitional stage in the evolution of birds from other theropods. The fossil is a mosaic of dinosaur and bird features. Like later birds, *Archaeopteryx* had wings and feathers. Unlike modern birds, *Archaeopteryx* had teeth and a long tail, two of the many traits linking it to theropod dinosaurs.

*Archaeopteryx,* now known from 10 specimens, is considered the earliest known bird, but it is not considered a direct ancestor of modern birds. Exactly how close *Archaeopteryx* is to modern birds is being debated. The recent discovery of a consider able variety of small, feathered dinosaurs that date from the Early Cretaceous of China is providing paleontologists with an abundance of fossil evidence to piece together the evolutionary connections between theropods and birds. This part of the dinosaur story will be explored later in this series.

## SUMMARY

This chapter described the continuing evolution of predatory dinosaurs during the Middle and Late Jurassic Epochs and the adaptations that led to their continued success.

1. Theropods, the predatory dinosaurs, were, like sauropods,
   saurischians, with a unique dinosaurian hip structure that
   enabled mobility and the evolution of large body sizes.

2. Theropods ranged in size from small, chicken-sized taxa to
   gigantic carnivores that measured upward of 50 feet (15 m)
   long.

3. Two theropod clades predominated during the Middle and
   Late Jurassic Epochs. The clade Ceratosauria includes the
   most primitive theropods. The basal Tetanurae includes the
   least derived nonceratosaurian theropods.

4. Basal tetanurans that lived during the Middle and Late Jurassic are divided into two subgroups: Spinosauridae, including
   megalosaurs, and Avetheropoda, including carnosaurs and
   coelurosaurs.

5. The best known carnosaur from the Late Jurassic is *Allosaurus*, which weighed up to three tons and measured about 40
   feet (12 m) long.

6. The existence of large predators such as *Allosaurus* and the
   later tyrannosaurs, spinosaurs, and carcharodontosaurs is
   evidence that prey animals such as iguanodonts, hadrosaurs,
   sauropods, and horned dinosaurs probably lived in great
   numbers and required predators to adapt highly specialized
   weapons and techniques to hunt them down.

7. The senses of vision, smell, and hearing were generally more
   acute in theropods than in prey animals; this helped to make
   the theropods effective predators.

8. The speeds of theropods are best understood by modeling their anatomy and musculature based on knowledge of
   extant animals. The top speed of *Tyrannosaurus* was probably
   between 10 and 25 mph (6 to 16 km/hr).

9. Three killing tactics used by theropods were grapple-and-slash, grapple-and-bite, and pursuit-and-bite techniques.

10. *Archaeopteryx* is the earliest known bird and represents a transitional stage in the evolution of birds from other dinosaurs. *Archaeopteryx* is not likely directly related to modern birds.

# ARMORED AND PLATED DINOSAURS: ORNITHISCHIAN INNOVATIONS

Ornithischian dinosaurs made up the other of the two major clades of dinosaurs, and that clade's members are united by a generalized morphology of the pelvis known as a "bird-like," or ornithischian, hip. As explained earlier, the group of theropods that includes birds and their ancestors independently evolved a very similar hip structure, although well after the ornithischian dinosaurs.

Ornithischians included a variety of bipedal and quadrupedal herbivores and were highly successful and specialized plant eaters; many of them grew to large size and lived in herds. The most common groups of ornithischian dinosaurs were the Stegosauria, or plated dinosaurs (Middle Jurassic to Early Cretaceous); the Ankylosauria, or armored dinosaurs (Middle Jurassic to Late Cretaceous); the Ornithopoda (Middle Jurassic to Late Cretaceous), including the Iguanodontia and the Hadrosauridae, or duck-billed dinosaurs (Late Cretaceous); the Pachycephalosauria, or bone-headed dinosaurs (Late Cretaceous); and the Ceratopsia, or horned dinosaurs (Late Jurassic to Late Cretaceous). Of these, the stegosaurs and ornithopods predominated in the Middle and Late Jurassic Epochs, the subject of *Time of the Giants*, although rare ankylosaurs and basal ceratopsians were around at that time, too.

This chapter describes the rise and diversification of the stegosaurs and ankylosaurs, two of the most unusual clades of dinosaurs due to their specialized plate and armor structures, adaptations for eating, and defensive weaponry. The remaining groups of diverse and populous ornithischians are fully described in *Last of the Dinosaurs.*

# EVOLUTION OF THE ORNITHISCHIANS

Fossils of ornithischians are rare until the Middle Jurassic. Their earliest representatives lived among the first saurischians of the Late Triassic but make only the scarcest of appearances in the fossil record. These early ornithischians were seemingly overshadowed by larger and more numerous saurischian meat eaters and plant eaters. Somehow, however, the small, herbivorous ornithischians persisted. They survived into the Jurassic Period and became the seeds of many great lines of later innovative and successful plant-eating dinosaurs.

Several anatomical features unite the ornithischians. Aside from having a similar hip structure, all ornithischians had a toothless beak on the upper jaw and an unusual, scooplike predentary bone at the tip of the lower jaw. Except for the most basal taxa, all ornithischians had cheeks to help prevent food from falling out of the mouth as the food was chewed. When combined with leaf-shaped cheek teeth and a variety of highly specialized dental adaptations for grinding vegetation, these features of the mouth eventually elevated the ornithischians to the summit of plant-eating effectiveness in the dinosaur world. Unlike the saurischians, whose skulls were lightened by many enlarged fenestrae or "windows," and whose vertebrae were sculpted for strength and lightness, the ornithischians' skulls had smaller fenestrae (in some species, some or all of the fenestrae were lost entirely during the course of evolution); additionally, the skeletons of ornithischians were generally heavier and more robust in comparison to their body mass. The ornithischian skull was sometimes armored, and all ornithischians had a characteristic bony knob or protuberance in the area of the eyelid.

The hip region of the ornithischian backbone had five or more fused sacral vertebrae for added strength. The fifth toe of the ornithischian foot was greatly reduced, as in sauropods and theropods, but this had little effect on the ornithischians' ability to walk or run. Most ornithischians were good runners, with the exception, perhaps, of the wide-bodied ankylosaurs.

The earliest members of the Ornithischia are shrouded in mystery due to the scarcity of their fossil remains. Some are known only from teeth. The best-known basal ornithischians are *Lesothosaurus* (Early Jurassic, Lesotho); *Pisanosaurus* (Late Triassic, Argentina); *Heterodontosaurus* (Early Jurassic, South Africa); *Stormbergia* (Early Jurassic, South Africa and Lesotho); and *Eocursor* (Late Triassic, South Africa). Uniting these early dinosaurs with the ornithischians were their possession of the classic ornithischian pelvis; leaf-shaped dentition in the cheek areas of the jaws; a bony beak (albeit a very small one, restricted only to the tip of the jaw); and a predentary bone. All three were small animals, about three feet (0.9 m) long. Paleontologist Michael Benton has pointed out that tooth wear seen in the jaw of *Lesothosaurus* suggests that the animal used an up-and-down chopping motion but had not yet adapted the backward-and-forward-plus-sideways jaw mobility that characterizes the chewing motion seen in later ornithischians. The mere evidence of chewing of any sort, however, establishes that even the earliest ornithischians were developing adaptations for processing food in the mouth that differed greatly from the feeding strategies seen in the sauropodomorphs. Improvements to the ornithischian dental battery are seen in stegosaurs and ankylosaurs but were carried to their greatest lengths in other lines of later ornithischians, such as the duck-billed and horned dinosaurs.

Stegosaurs and ankylosaurs belong to a larger clade called Thyreophora, or "shield bearers." All members of this group were quadrupedal, had some form of body armor or plating, and were widely distributed geographically. The armor plating ranged from small bony nodes to large plates and spikes that were embedded in the skin and ran in rows along the back and sides; some even had armor on their faces, arms, and legs.

Thyreophorans shared a common ancestor. Some basal members of the clade were neither stegosaurs nor ankylosaurs. The three best-understood basal thyreophorans are *Scuttellosaurus* (Early Jurassic, Arizona); *Emausaurus* (Early Jurassic, Germany); and *Scelidosaurus* (Early Jurassic, England). All three were small to medium-sized herbivores that measured from 3.5 to 13.5 feet (1 to 4 m) long and were primarily quadrupedal.

Of these basal thyreophorans, spectacularly well-preserved specimens of *Scelidosaurus* with armor *in situ* (found intact in its original place of deposition) provide the best evidence of the placement of bony plating on the body of early ornithischians. The armor of *Scelidosaurus* consisted largely of small oval nodes, or **scutes**, made of bone. Some smaller plates were mere knobs, while the largest were round, with stout ridges. Plates were arranged in several rows along the spine and on the sides of the animal. The tail had four rows along its lateral and dorsal surfaces. The base of the neck was protected by triangular-shaped plates. Small plates along the spine were firmly attached to the skeleton through ligaments fastened to the vertebrae. Although many fossil scutes of various sizes have been associated with the remains of *Scutellosaurus* and *Emausaurus*, the jumbled condition of the remains of those dinosaurs makes it difficult to ascertain the pattern of the armor; as in all later thyreophorans, however, it likely was arranged in rows that paralleled the length of the body.

## STEGOSAURIA: TRAITS AND DIVERSITY

The "plated" dinosaurs, or Stegosauria, were among the first thyreophorans to appear; the others were ankylosaurs. The earliest stegosaur fossils have been found in China and date from the Middle Jurassic, about 170 million years ago. There were two clades of stegosaurs, the Huayangosauridae and the Stegosauridae. All members of the Stegosauria shared several defining traits, including small, narrow heads; heavy, short forelimbs; long, robust hind limbs; and sturdy feet that bore hooflike bones on the ends of the

*Stegosaurus*

toes. All stegosaurs bore some form of vertical, bony plates or spikes that were raised up and attached in a double row along the back.

*Huayangosauridae.* The earliest stegosaurs are represented by only one member, *Huayangosaurus* ("Huayang lizard"). *Huayangosaurus* is known from one complete skeleton with a skull and from several partial skeletons; this makes it one of the best-known early ornithischian dinosaurs. *Huayangosaurus* differed from members of the Stegosauridae in several ways. Measuring about 14 feet (4.3 m) long, it was somewhat smaller than the stegosaurs of the Late Jurassic and Early Cretaceous. Its skull was taller and had a shorter snout, with eyes positioned more forward than in members of the Stegosauridae. *Huayangosaurus* had seven teeth in its **premaxilla**, the front-most bone of the upper jaw that was toothless in other kinds of stegosaurs. Its armor consisted of a series of small plates and spikes along its back, and a tail equipped with a cluster of four sharp prongs with which to protect itself. One other significant difference between *Huayangosaurus* and other stegosaurs was that its front legs were nearly the same length as its hind limbs, an anatomical trait not seen in later stegosaurs, which have longer hind limbs.

*Stegosauridae.* All known stegosaurs other than *Huayangosaurus* are placed in this group. The Stegosauria consisted of medium- to large-sized plant eaters measuring from 10 to 30 feet (3 to 9 m) in length. Although once categorized by scientists as part of the group of armored dinosaurs that includes the Ankylosauria, the Stegosauria have now been distinguished from other armored dinosaurs by their skull morphology, tail weaponry, and lack of extensive body armor.

*Stegosaurus* is one of the most iconic of dinosaurs. With its distinctive row of back plates, tiny head, and impressive tail spikes, *Stegosaurus* illustrates many of the now-familiar traits of this unusual group of dinosaurs. When it was first described by Othniel C. Marsh, in 1877, *Stegosaurus* was an extraordinary discovery and the first well-known representative of the plated dinosaurs. Its fame spread quickly due largely to a magnificent and nearly complete specimen extracted in Colorado by Marsh's fossil collectors in 1886. The traits seen in the first specimens of *Stegosaurus* went far in defining the characteristics of this clade:

- Quadrupedal stance with a body that was highest at the hips because the animal had shorter forelimbs than hind limbs.
- Two rows of vertical plates or spikes running from the base of the neck down the back and onto the tail. These varied in size and were largest over the back and hip region. In *Stegosaurus*, these armor plates consisted of 17 thin, upright plates, no two of the same exact shape or size. The plates were positioned in two alternating rows along the back of the animal. Other stegosaurs had similar arrangements of the back plates, although they were usually smaller and found in different numbers than in *Stegosaurus*. *Tuojiangosaurus* (Late Jurassic, China) had a row of robust spines along its back, and *Kentrosaurus* (Late Jurassic, Tanzania) had a row of narrow plates on the neck and shoulders that turned

into long, sharp spikes that continued from the top of its back to the tip of its tail and measured about 2 feet (60 cm) long. In addition, some species, such as *Gigantspinosaurus* (Late Jurassic, China), had huge, backward curving spikes protruding from the shoulders.

- Stegosaur tails had two pairs of defensive spikes pointing outward to the sides and a bit upward and backward.
- Stegosaur skulls were typically long, squat, and narrow, with toothless beaks and small, triangular, ridged teeth in the cheek regions.
- Stegosaur tails were not particularly as well stiffened as those of other ornithischians. This may have affected the stegosaurs' mobility because a stiff tail enabled some dinosaurs to keep better balance when they ran. The stegosaurs' sturdy, heavy skeleton, short front legs, and inflexible limbs and feet probably gave them a stiffened gait similar to that of an elephant.
- Some stegosaurs had additional armor, in the form of small bony knobs, or **ossicles**, protecting their throats and sides. The ossicles were tightly packed, like the chain mail in a suit of armor.

The function of the back plates of stegosaurs has been a source of debate, particularly for *Stegosaurus*, which exhibits the largest and flattest example of plates of all the stegosaurs. The plates originally were thought to provide protection; at least one early view (formed before a good, articulated skeleton was discovered) was that the plates lay flat on the back like shingles on a roof.

Close examination of the anatomy of *Stegosaurus* plates reveals that they were not rock solid in real life but rich with blood vessels, both on their surfaces and internally. As a means of armor protection, such plates were no match for the bone-crunching teeth of a large predatory dinosaur and didn't cover much of the body, either. The visually stunning appearance of the plates, however, could have given the stegosaur the appearance of a much larger animal, making it more threatening to a potential attacker. As a means of display, the plates could have played a role in distinguishing one species from another and, within a species, one individual from another—a useful feature when vying for a mate. It is even possible that the rich blood supply in the plates allowed stegosaurs to change the color of their plates at will, much as a chameleon does today, thus suggesting a kind of billboard for attracting a member of the opposite sex.

Aside from their visual appeal, stegosaur back plates were probably excellent conductors of heat. The flow of blood that permeated the plates would have made them an effective heat-exchange system. Heat would have been dissipated from the plates during hot weather and gathered for absorption by the dinosaur in cool weather. It should also be noted that the thermoregulatory function of stegosaur back plates is restricted to *Stegosaurus,* which had large, flat, vascularized plates. Most stegosaurs lacked such plates and instead were adorned with bony spikes and spines that probably served as visual displays rather than heat conductors. This suggests that the heat transfer function of *Stegosaurus* plates, if indeed the animal utilized them for this purpose, was a relatively unimportant secondary function that did not evolve in other stegosaurs.

## The Brain of a *Stegosaurus*

While the intelligence of dinosaurs cannot be discerned with any certainty from the fossil record, *Stegosaurus* certainly ranked among the least brainy of known dinosaurs. The size of its brain, estimated to be about that of a walnut, was on the lowest end of a ratio comparing brain size to body mass in dinosaurs. Only sauropods and ankylosaurs had smaller brains. So startling was this fact that well-meaning scientists looked elsewhere for an answer to *Stegosaurus* intelligence.

When Marsh first examined the skeleton of *Stegosaurus,* he noticed that in addition to its small braincase, the rear section of the spine contained a "very large chamber . . . formed by an enlargement of the spinal canal" inside the vertebrae of the hips. He noted that this "suggestive subject" might lead one to believe that the creature had an auxiliary brain in its rear end, an idea that quickly caught the public's attention. *Stegosaurus* became known as the dinosaur with two brains—one for its front and one for its rear. In actuality, the cavity in the backbone of *Stegosaurus* was no more than a widening in the nerve canal. The same kind of cavity has since been observed in sauropods, birds, and many land vertebrates and is never occupied by a "second brain." In birds, the extra space is taken up by a structure known as a glycogen body. The glycogen body appears to supply a reserve of carbohydrates to the nervous system to help nerve fibers grow. Whether stegosaurs (or any other dinosaurs) had glycogen bodies is not known, but it is an intriguing possibility.

## ANKYLOSAURIA: TRAITS AND DIVERSITY

The armored dinosaurs, or Ankylosauria, first appeared in the Middle Jurassic Epoch. The name Ankylosauria, meaning "fused lizard," refers to the fact that in the Late Cretaceous *Ankylosaurus*, the first named ankylosaur, small armor plates appear fused to the skull, and some of the ribs are fused to the vertebrae in the back. Ankylosaurs were bulky, quadrupedal herbivores with highly specialized body armor. Some taxa were literally the size of tanks, reaching lengths of 33 feet (10 m). Armored dinosaurs are divided into two groups, the Ankylosauridae and the Nodosauridae.

Common traits shared by all ankylosaurs include skull armor; closed fenestrae in front of the eyes and on top of the skull; small heads with noninterlocking, spatula-shaped teeth; widely arched ribs that accentuated a broad body covered with extensive armor scutes and spikes; robust legs; and forelimbs that were shorter than the hind limbs. To accommodate their heavy body armor, the ribs and pelvic bones of ankylosaurs were broadened and strengthened to provide a firm base to which body armor and massive muscles could be affixed.

Ankylosaurs and nodosaurs were tallest at the hips. Their stocky legs were adapted for carrying their heavy weight. The limbs of

*Euoplocephalus* (foreground) and *Edmontia*

nodosaurs were a little lighter than those of ankylosaurs, but members of both clades were slow moving and probably not as fast as other quadrupedal ornithischians such as the horned dinosaurs.

The oldest known, unambiguous ankylosaur was *Gargoylesaurus* (Late Jurassic, Wyoming), a small specimen known from a small skull and partial skeleton. At least two less well understood ankylosaur specimens, *Dracopelta* (Late Jurassic, Portugal) and *Mymoorapelta* (Late Jurassic, Colorado) suggest that the rise of armored dinosaurs was already in full swing during the heyday of the sauropods and stegosaurs. Definitive specimens of nodosaurids do not appear until the Early Cretaceous and include *Sauropelta* from Montana, *Cedarpelta* from Utah, and *Pawpawsaurus* from Texas. Both groups of armored dinosaurs outlasted the stegosaurs, which disappeared by the end of the Early Cretaceous, and both groups were still thriving near the time of the final extinction of the dinosaurs.

Remains of ankylosaurs have been found in both the Northern and Southern Hemispheres, but they were largely a Northern Hemisphere phenomenon, with extraordinary specimens coming from China, Mongolia, and western North America. A few specimens have also been found in Europe, South America, Australia, and Antarctica.

*Ankylosauridae.* These earliest members of the armored dinosaurs bore wide, triangular armored skulls and had massive clubs on the end of their tails. Head armor formed a mosaic of thick, bony plates that were fused to the skull. The dorsal surface of the head was completely armor covered, including bony studs around the eyes. *Euoplocephalus* (Late Cretaceous, Montana and Alberta) had the additional protection of a bony, retractable eyelid. Body armor consisted of small spines, bony knobs, long spikes, and flat and rounded scutes of various sizes. The side of the skull was protected by stout, bony prongs at the rear corners. The snout and skull of the most advanced ankylosaurs had a complex network of air chambers through which the animals breathed. These nasal passages improved their sense of smell and possibly acted as a resonating chamber for making sounds.

The armor plates of ankylosaurids and nodosaurids were normally arranged in bands along the neck, back, and tail. In some cases, the armor was embellished by knobs and spines, especially on the back. The space between individual scutes was filled with a matrix of smaller scutes or bony ossicles. The ankylosaur for which there is the most fossil evidence is *Euoplocephalus* ("well armored head"), a moderately large armored dinosaur that measured about 23 feet (7 m) long. The topside of this animal was completely protected by a bony mosaic of scutes from the tip of its nose to its bony tail club.

*Ankylosaurus,* from the Late Cretaceous of Montana and Alberta, is one of the largest and most famous ankylosaurs. It was certainly the largest known, measuring up to 33 feet (10 m) and probably weighing up to four tons (3.6 metric tons). The tail club alone,

*Ankylosaurus* tail club

consisting of a massive bony knob weighing more than 110 pounds (50 kg), was a lethal weapon if swung accurately at the head or legs of an attacking predator.

Several ankylosaurs, including *Gastonia* (Early Cretaceous, Utah) and *Polacanthus* (Early Cretaceous, England and Spain), are notable because they represent anatomic mosaics of ankylosaurid and nodosaurid traits. *Gastonia* had a heavily armored body and is known from the fossil remains of two complete and two partial skulls and five partial skeletons. Its body armor and skull most resemble those of other ankylosaurids. *Gastonia*, however, also had robust spikes lining its sides, and it lacked a tail club, two characteristics of the nodosaurids. It is possible that *Gastonia* and *Polacanthus* represent a third clade of Ankylosauria.

*Nodosauridae.* Nodosaurids differed from ankylosaurids in several respects. They did not have tail clubs, and their body armor

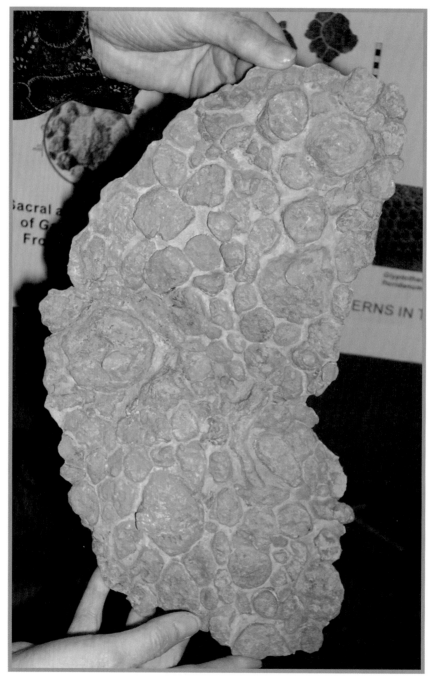

Body armor of the ankylosaur *Gastonia*

*Sauropelta*

often combined large spikes, particularly lining the sides of the body, with armored plates made up of smaller bony tiles or scutes. The head was narrower and not as heavily armored as in the ankylosaurids. Nodosaurid skulls did not have bony horns at the back corners of the head as did the ankylosaurids. Nodosaurids had sturdy limbs like ankylosaurids and moved at a slow pace.

The nodosaurid *Edmontonia* had several bands of very large scutes crossing its back from side to side. The largest were over the shoulders and were six- or eight-sided, with sharp ridges down their centers. The back armor of the nodosaurid *Sauropelta* consisted of smaller knobby scutes than those of *Edmontonia*, but the scutes on *Sauropelta* were thicker and had a point or ridge.

Members of the heavily armored Ankylosauria must have been the most frustrating of all prey for a theropod. What the nodosaurids lacked in a tail club, they gained in the presence of more—and large—upward-pointing spikes and horny knobs. The shoulder areas of nodosaurids shows evidence of strong muscles, more so than in ankylosaurs. This suggests that nodosaurs actively defended themselves by lunging forward and swinging their shoulders back and forth, bringing into play an abundance of spikes and protective armor in the anterior part of the body. Their powerful gait, formidable armor, and threatening body spikes represented serious danger to any attacking predator. Having said that, it should be noted that as with antelope horns or deer antlers, while such body spikes *can* be used defensively, their *primary* function was probably for intraspecies displays or combat for mates and territory.

## STEGOSAURIA AND ANKYLOSAURIA FEEDING

The armored and plated dinosaurs were all low-browsing animals, picking plants from ground cover, bushes, and other material at the base of the flora. They ate below the line of plants normally consumed by the taller sauropods and iguanodontians. They probably plowed into the vegetation with their sharp beaks, snipping off branches and twigs with a snap of the jaws and a sideways pull of the head.

The herbivorous stegosaurs and ankylosaurs were equipped with simple but effective jaws and teeth. The teeth were inset from the edges of the jaws, forming significant ridges of bone on the upper and lower jaws that protruded quite a bit from the location of the teeth; this suggests that these creatures had fleshy cheeks in which to hold food that was being chewed. The animals' spatula- or leaf-shaped teeth were set in rows and were well suited for tearing vegetation rather than grinding it. As in the sauropods, the breakdown of food was probably done in the stomach and gut. Stegosaurs and especially the ankylosaurs had huge guts in which the natural digestive fermentation of food took place slowly but effectively.

Plant life on Earth changed dramatically during the rise and evolution of these dinosaurs. Three major kinds of land plants were common during the Jurassic and Cretaceous Periods in which the stegosaurs and ankylosaurs lived. Their diet may have consisted in part of the following menu.

*Pteridophytes.* These included the ferns. Ferns grew in forms that hugged the ground but also grew as trees, with a single unadorned, stemlike trunk and a single growing point at the top. These plants generally required a moist environment. They were fast growing and so could be grazed without being killed; this made them an excellent renewable source of food. Pteridophytes were abundant throughout the age of dinosaurs. They were an especially important source of food for lower-browsing armored and plated dinosaurs.

*Equisetopsids.* These include horsetails and scouring rushes. Their leaves are greatly reduced, and the stems are jointed and photosynthetic. Some early species were trees measuring more than 100 feet (30 m) tall.

*Gymnosperms.* There were, and are, many different kinds of seed plants, but during the Mesozoic, two groups, the conifers and the cycads, were among the most abundant. They reproduced by means of a "naked seed," in contrast to the seeds of angiosperms, which are enclosed within a fruit. Other branches of the conifer group include the cypress and bald cypress. In contrast to the conifers, the cycads were mostly short plants with bulbous or palmlike trunks, although they also had some treelike forms. They were capped with fronds reminiscent of palm trees. Gymnosperms were neither moist nor soft forms of vegetation; they were not an easy food to digest. They were gradually displaced as a source of food by the rise of the flowering plants, or angiosperms, in the Cretaceous Period.

*Angiosperms.* These are flowering plants, the last of the major plant groups to evolve. They are distinguished by having a seed borne within a fruit, unlike the gymnosperms, which bear naked seeds. Angiosperms first appeared in the Early Cretaceous but did not begin to become common until the Late Cretaceous. This means that only the later Cretaceous thyreophorans really had to deal with angiosperms; Middle and Late Jurassic thyreophorans contented themselves with gymnosperms, pteridophytes, and other plants. Angiosperms diversified and spread rapidly in the form of flowering shrubs to become the dominant plant group by the end of the

Cretaceous. Angiosperms reproduced and grew more quickly than gymnosperms this made them abundantly available as dinosaur food. The foliage of most angiosperms was generally more digestible, moist, and nutritionally sound than that of either pteridophytes or gymnosperms. The ability of these plants to spread and grow quickly made them ideally suited for food for herbivores.

## SUMMARY

This chapter described the rise and diversification of the stegosaurs and ankylosaurs.

1. Ornithischian dinosaurs made up one of the two major clades of dinosaurs and included a variety of bipedal and quadrupedal herbivores. Ornithischians were highly specialized plant eaters, many of which grew to large size and lived in herds.

2. The first widely successful groups of ornithischians were the Stegosauria, or plated dinosaurs, and the Ankylosauria, the armored dinosaurs. Stegosaurs and ankylosaurs belong to a larger clade called Thyreophora, or "shield bearers." All members of the group were quadrupedal, had leaf-shaped cheek teeth for tearing vegetation, had some form of body armor or plating, and were widely distributed geographically.

3. The earliest stegosaur fossils have been found in China and date from the Middle Jurassic. All stegosaurs had small, narrow heads and heavy limbs and bore some form of vertical, bony plates or spikes running in a double row along the back. Some grew up to 30 feet (9 m) long.

4. The large, triangular back plates of *Stegosaurus* served as a visual display for warding off predators or attracting the attention of a potential mate. The plates were highly vascular and may also have served as heat conductors for raising or lowering the body temperature of the dinosaur.

5. The armored dinosaurs, or Ankylosauria, first appeared in the Middle Jurassic. Some Cretaceous taxa reached lengths of 33 feet (10 m).

6. Armored dinosaurs are divided into two families, the Ankylosauridae and the Nodosauridae. Ankylosaurids had broader, more heavily armored heads and massive tail clubs for protection. Nodosaurids had narrower skulls and lacked tail clubs but were adorned with a variety of spikes, bony knobs and armor plates. Both groups of armored dinosaurs were slow-moving creatures.

7. The ankylosaur for which there is the most evidence is *Euoplocephalus* ("true armored head"), a moderately large armored dinosaur measuring about 23 feet (7 m) long. The topside of this animal was completely protected by a bony mosaic of scutes from the tip of its nose to its bony tail club.

8. Stegosaurs and ankylosaurs probably used their tail spikes, clubs, and body spikes to defend themselves against predators.

9. The herbivorous stegosaurs and ankylosaurs were equipped with simple but effective jaws and teeth. They were grazing and low-browsing animals, picking plants from ground cover, bushes, and other material at the base of the herbivory.

# Conclusion

The Middle and Late Jurassic Epochs were populated by some of the best-known and most spectacular dinosaurs. The gigantic sauropods—including *Apatosaurus*, *Diplodocus*, and *Camarasaurus*—were among the first of the long-necked titans discovered and described based on fossils found when American fossil hunters entered the rich fossil beds of western North America during the 1870s. For many years, those very first specimens symbolized everything that was dinosaurian in the public's view. The discovery of sauropods was soon followed by the excavation of large and equally spectacular predatory dinosaurs such as *Allosaurus*. Then the first specimen of *Stegosaurus* was found, further detailing a distantly remote time when animals the size of small buildings walked the Earth and fought for their survival with size, girth, teeth, talons, and spikes in seemingly unending varieties.

The early discovery of sauropods, large theropods, and stegosaurs created an impression of dinosaurs as monstrous, stupid, and lumbering lizards. Since that time, the continued discovery and study of many more dinosaur specimens have provided a wealth of new data and interpretations. The scientific view of dinosaurs as living creatures has changed greatly during the past 150 years. Once considered docile and inactive like their distant, "cold-blooded" reptilian relatives, dinosaurs now are thought to have been active, energetic creatures that used a variety of thermoregulatory schemes to maintain a constant body temperature. Close examination of the fossil evidence coupled with observations about the living habits of extant creatures have also provided a better informed view of the probable lifestyles of dinosaurs.

By the end of the Jurassic Period, many important trends in the evolution of dinosaurs had taken place. Sauropods represented extremism in the size of land animals, with equally elegant metabolic and thermoregulatory schemes to maintain active lifestyles. Theropods were evolving along several different paths, some large and some small. Other creatures, such as *Archaeopteryx*, began the earliest experimentation of dinosaurs with powered flight, presaging the rise of birds. Among the ornithischians, the plated and armored dinosaurs developed sophisticated jaws and teeth that represented advances in the abilities of herbivorous dinosaurs to chew their food. Equally compelling was their armor plating and weaponry, traits that would persist in their descendants throughout the remaining years of the Mesozoic that followed.

By the end of the Jurassic Period, several evolutionary trends were in motion that would be played out by dinosaurs in the second half of the Mesozoic Era. Sauropods would continue their domination of the high-browsing herbivory, spreading and diversifying in numerous ways to all corners of the globe. Theropods would proliferate with great variation in small, medium, and large sizes, leading to the largest terrestrial predators of all time, such as *Tyrannosaurus*. Equally important, however, was the evolution of a small line of theropods that led directly to powered flight and the emergence of birds. The ornithischians would expand in the greatest numbers during the Cretaceous Period. Joining the ankylosaurs would be a wide range of herbivores, including the iguanodontians and horned dinosaurs.

The success of the dinosaurs for so many years is astounding. They existed in one form or another for more than 160 million years. Humans, by comparison, exist today only as a single species that first arose from the evolutionary stock of primates about 2 million years ago. Modern-type humans arose a mere 200,000 years ago. Yet it is not the longevity of the dinosaurs that makes them so popular. When a child is asked why he or she likes dinosaurs, a common reply is that dinosaurs are "big, scary, and dead." Paleontologists are equally passionate about these lost creatures. In the earliest days of dinosaur hunting in the American West, when Edward Drinker Cope first made some of his most startling dinosaur discoveries, he wrote home to his young daughter Julia about his finds:

> *I have found four new kinds of Laelaps [a dinosaur] which ate meat and several kinds that ate leaves and wood. They were as large as elephants and their teeth are very small, no larger than the end of my little finger. One kind had more than 400 in his mouth at once, of which 100 were in use at once and the rest coming on from below to take their places as soon as they were worn out.*

In 1876, when Cope wrote this, one could count the number of known dinosaur genera on the fingers of one's hands. Cope and his rival, Othniel Charles Marsh, were about to open up a wide new window onto the mysteries of prehistoric life. The enthusiasm and relish with which these men attacked their work still resonates in the science of dinosaurs.

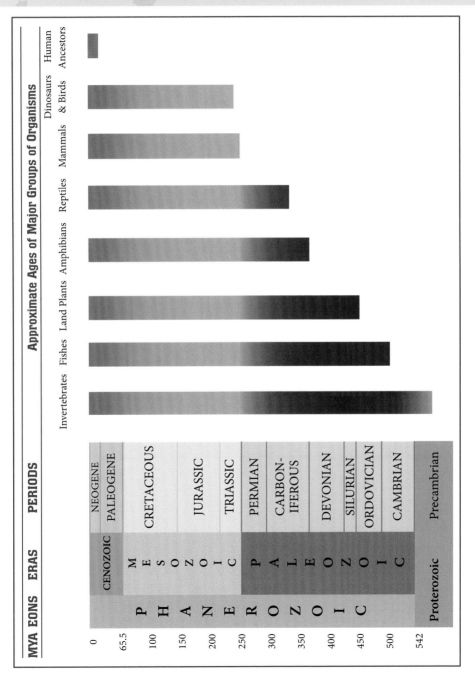

# APPENDIX TWO:
# POSITIONAL TERMS

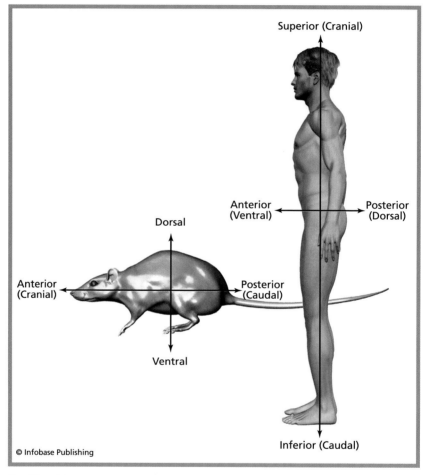

Positional terms used to describe vertebrate anatomy

# GLOSSARY

**acetabulum**  In a vertebrate, a socket in the pelvic girdle to which the leg bones are connected.

**adaptations**  Anatomical, physiological, and behavioral changes that occur in an organism that enable it to survive environmental changes.

**anatomy**  The collective basic biological systems of an animal, such as the skeletal and muscular systems.

**anterior**  Directional term meaning toward the head, or cranial, end of a vertebrate.

**anterior process**  A forward-pointing extension of the pubis bone.

**antorbital fenestra**  In the archosaurian skull, an additional opening in the side of the skull positioned just in front of the orbit, or eye opening.

**Archosauria**  The branch of diapsid reptiles including dinosaurs, pterosaurs, crocodiles, birds and their kin.

**articulated skeleton**  A fossil skeleton found with its bones in place, connected as they would have been in life.

**Avetheropoda**  Division of the Theropoda including Carnosauria and Coelurosauria.

**basal**  At or near the base or earliest level of evolutionary development; a term usually used to refer to ancestral taxon.

**binocular vision**  Overlapping vision of the two eyes.

**bone bed**  Fossil locality with a high concentration of bones from more than one individual.

**bradymetabolism**  A slow resting metabolic process.

**braincase**  A protective portion of the skull containing the brain cavity and nerve connections to the brain.

**carnivorous**  Meat-eating.

**centrum**  The spool-shaped supporting structure at the center of a vertebra.

**chevron**  A bony, downward-pointing bone that occurs on the underside of a tail vertebra, the function of which was muscle attachment.

**clade**   A group of related organisms including all the descendants of a single common ancestor.

**cladistic analysis**   An analytical technique for comparing the genetic, morphological, and behavioral traits of taxa.

**climate**   The kind of weather that occurs at a particular place over time.

**clutch**   Group of eggs in a nest.

**coevolution**   A change, through natural selection, in the genetic makeup of one species in response to a genetic change in another.

**derived**   Term used to describe a trait of an organism that is a departure from the basal (ancestral) form.

**diagnostic trait**   A measurable feature in the morphology of a fossil that can be used to identify members of a given clade or taxon of extinct animal.

**Diapsida reptiles**   Amniotes with two temporal fenestrae, a lower one like the one seen in synapsids and a second one on top the skull and behind the orbit.

**dinosaur**   Member of a clade of extinct ornithodiran archosaurian reptiles with an upright posture and either a saurischian or ornithischian style of hip.

**Dinosauriformes**   Member of a clade of ornithodirans more closely related to dinosaurs than to pterosaurs.

**dispersalist biogeography**   A theory of animal distribution that takes into account the migration of organisms from one continent to another via land bridges.

**ectothermic**   Term used to describe a "cold-blooded" vertebrate.

**endothermic**   Term used to describe a "warm-blooded" vertebrate.

**era**   A span of geologic time ranking below the eon; the Archean Eon is divided into four eras dating from more than 4 billion years ago to 2.5 billion years ago; the Proterozoic Eon is divided into three eras dating from 2.5 billion years ago to about 542 million years ago; the Phanerozoic Eon is divided into three eras, the Paleozoic, the Mesozoic, and the Cenozoic; the Paleozoic ("ancient life") Era lasted from 542 million to 251 million years ago; the Mesozoic ("middle life") Era lasted from 251 million to 65.5 million years ago; the Cenozoic ("recent life") Era began 65.5 million years ago and continues to the present.

**evolution**   The natural process by which species gradually change over time, controlled by changes to the genetic code—the DNA—of organisms and whether or not those changes enable an organism to survive in a given environment.

**extant**   Term used to describe an organism that is living today; not extinct.

**extinction**   The irreversible elimination of an entire species of organism because it cannot adapt effectively to changes in its environment.

**fauna**   Animals found in a given ecosystem.

**femur**   Upper hind limb bone.

**fibula**   Outermost lower leg bone.

**flora**   Plants found in a given ecosystem.

**forelimbs**   The two front legs of a vertebrate.

**fossil**   Any physical trace or remains of prehistoric life.

**gastroliths**   Stones swallowed by an animal, often to aid in the crushing and processing of food once it has been swallowed.

**gene**   A portion of a DNA strand that controls a particular inherited trait.

**genus**   (plural: genera) A taxonomic name for one or more closely related organisms that is divided into species; names of organisms, such as *Tyrannosaurus rex*, are composed of two parts, the genus name (first) and the species name (second).

**geographic isolation**   The isolation of species on a land formation as a result of naturally occurring geologic events (e.g., the formation of an island or of mountains).

**gigantism**   Unusually large inherited growth traits for a taxon made possible through natural selection.

**gigantothermy**   A thermoregulatory process found in vertebrates that combines low metabolic rate, large body mass, and a circulatory system for radiating blood outward toward body tissues.

**Gondwana**   Name given to Earth's southern landmass during the Mesozoic Era; formed by the breakup of Pangaea, Gondwana included regions that would become the continents of South America, Africa, India, Australia, and Antarctica.

**herbivore**   An animal whose primary food source is vegetation.

**heterodont**   Having different kinds of teeth in different zones of the jaw.

**hind limbs**   The two rear legs of a vertebrate.

**homeothermy**   The moderation of core body temperature due to large body mass.

**humerus**   Upper bone of the forelimb.

***in situ***   "In place," as in a fossil found intact in its original location of deposition.

**ilium**   (plural: ilia) The uppermost bone of the pelvis that is connected to the backbone.

**ischium**   In a vertebrate, a pelvic bone located below and behind the acetabulum.

**Laurasia**   Name given to Earth's northern landmass during the Mesozoic Era; formed by the breakup of Pangaea, Laurasia included regions that would become the continents of North America, Europe, and Asia.

**Lepidosauria**   A group of diapsid reptiles that includes lizards, snakes, and two species of *Sphenodon*—the lizardlike tuatara of New Zealand—and their extinct kin.

**mass extinction**   An extinction event that kills off more than 25 percent of all species in a million years or less.

**maxilla**   Major tooth-bearing bone of the upper jaw.

**metabolism**   The combination of all biochemical processes that take place in an organism to keep it alive.

**monophyletic**   A natural clade of animals descended from a common ancestor.

**morphological**   Pertaining to the body form and structure of an organism.

**natural selection**   One of Charles Darwin's observations regarding the way evolution works: Given the complex and changing conditions under which life exists, those individuals with the combination of inherited traits best suited to a particular environment will survive and reproduce while others will not.

**neural arch**   Part of a vertebra above the centrum that forms a protective sheath around the nerve cord.

**neural spine**   A bony, upward-pointing process on a vertebra, the function of which was muscle attachment.

**olfactory**   Related to the sense of smell.

**optic**   Related to the sense of vision.

**Ornithischia**   One of the two clades of dinosaurs; characterized by a "bird-hipped" pelvis.

**otic**   related to the sense of hearing

**ossicle**   A small, bony node on the skin; ossicles can form armored skin.

**otic**   Related to the sense of hearing.

**paleobiogeography**   A discipline of science whose goal is to explain the distribution of extinct organisms.

**paleontologist**   A scientist who studies prehistoric life, usually using fossils.

**Pangaea**   Earth's major landmass that formed during the Permian Period and lasted until the end of the Triassic Period and that later broke apart into two smaller landmasses, Laurasia and Gondwana.

**Panthalassic Ocean**   The ocean that bounded Pangaea on the west.

**paraphyletic**   A clade of organisms consisting of a common ancestor but *not* all the descendants of that ancestor.

**period**   A span of geologic time ranking below the era; the Phanerozoic Eon is divided into three eras and 11 periods, each covering a span of millions of years; the longest of these periods, including the three in the Mesozoic Era, are further broken down into smaller divisions of time (epochs).

**phylogeny**   The family tree of a group of related organisms, based on evolutionary history.

**physiology**   The way in which an animal's parts work together and are adapted to help the organism survive.

**pneumaticity**   A morphological feature of the vertebrae of some dinosaurs; the vertebrae show concavities and sculpted spaces that lightened the body without sacrificing strength; pneumaticity may be related to the presence of air sacs throughout the body to distribute oxygen to tissues.

**poikilothermy**   The inability to regulate a steady body temperature or metabolic process.

**population**   Members of the same species that live in a particular area.

**postcranial**   "Behind the head"; term generally used to refer to the portion of the vertebrate skeleton other than the head.

**posterior**   Directional term meaning toward the tail end; also known as the caudal end.

**predator**   An animal that actively seeks, kills, and feeds on other animals.

**premaxilla**   The forward-most, often tooth-bearing portion of the upper jaw of most vertebrates.

**pubis**   Hip bone located below and in front of the acetabulum.

**sacral vertebrae**   Vertebrae that are fused to the pelvis.

**sacrum**   A vertebral unit consisting of several, often fused, vertebrae that supports an ilium on each side.

**Saurischia**    One of the two clades of dinosaurs; characterized by a "lizard-hipped" pelvis.

**Sauropoda**    Clade of long-necked, usually large, herbivorous dinosaurs.

**Sauropodomorpha**    Clade of archosaurs that includes "prosauropod" and sauropod dinosaurs.

**scute**    A bony node located on the skin of an armored dinosaur; a flat-lying armor plate; larger than an ossicle.

**sexual dimorphism**    Variation in morphology between the males and females of a species.

**species**    In classification, the most basic biological unit of living organisms; members of a species can interbreed and produce fertile offspring.

**Spinosauroidea**    A superfamily of tetanuran theropod dinosaurs.

**Synapsida reptiles**    Amniotes with one temporal fenestra positioned somewhat behind and below the orbit.

**tachymetabolism**    A fast resting metabolic process.

**taxon**    (plural: taxa) In classification, a group of related organisms, such as a clade, genus, or species.

**temporal fenestrae**    Openings or "windows" in the vertebrate skull, just behind the orbit on the side and/or top of the skull (the temple region).

**Tethys Ocean**    The ocean that bounded Pangaea on the east.

**Theropoda**    Clade of archosaurs including all carnivorous, and some secondarily herbivorous, dinosaurs.

**tibia**    Innermost lower leg bone.

**topography**    Geologic character (elevation differences) of Earth's crust.

**trackway**    Series of sequential animal footprints.

**transitional**    Representing one step in the many stages that exist as species evolve.

**ungual**    An outermost bone of the toes and fingers.

**vicariance biogeography**    A theory stating that organisms are distributed geographically by riding on the backs of moving continents.

# CHAPTER BIBLIOGRAPHY

## Preface

Wilford, John Noble "When No One Read, Who Started to Write?"
*New York Times*, April, 6, 1999. Available online. URL: http://query.
nytimes.com/gst/fullpage.html?res=9B01EFD61139F935A35757C0A9
6F958260. Accessed October 22, 2007.

## Chapter 1 – The Middle and Late Jurassic Epochs

Berner, Robert A. "Atmospheric Oxygen Over Phanerozoic Time."
*Proceedings of the National Academy of Sciences of the United States of
America* 96, no. 20 (September 28, 1999): 10955–10957.

Chumakov, N.M. "Trends in Global Climate Changes Inferred from
Geological Data." *Stratigraphy and Geological Correlation* 12, no. 2
(2004): 7–32.

Ellis, Richard. *No Turning Back: The Life and Death of Animal Species.*
New York: Harper Collins, 2004.

Kious, W. Jacquelyne, and Robert I. Tilling. *This Dynamic Earth: The
Story of Plate Tectonics.* Washington: United States Geological Survey,
2001.

Morgans, Helen S., and Stephen P. Hesselbo. "The Seasonal Climate
of the Early-Middle Jurassic, Cleveland Basin, England." *Palaios* 14
(1999): 261–272.

Palmer, Douglas. *Atlas of the Prehistoric World.* New York: Discovery
Books, 1999.

Raup, David M. *Extinction: Bad Genes or Bad Luck?* New York: W.W.
Norton, 1991.

Rees, Peter McAllister, Alfred M. Ziegler, and Paul J. Valdes. *Jurassic
Phytogeography and Climates: New Data and Model Comparisons.*
Cambridge: Cambridge University Press, 2000.

———, Christopher R. Noto, J. Michael Parrish, and Judith T. Parrish.
"Late Jurassic Climates, Vegetation, and Dinosaur Distributions."
*Journal of Geology* 112 (2004): 643–653.

Ross, Charles A., George T. Moore, and Darryl N. Hayashida. "Late Jurassic Paleoclimate Simulation—Paleoecological Implications for Ammonoid Provinciality." *Palaios* 7 (1992): 487–507.

Saltzman, Barry. *Dynamical Paleoclimatology: Generalized Theory of Global Climate Change*, New York: Academic Press, 2002.

Weishampel, David B., Peter Dodson, and Halszka Osmólska, eds. *The Dinosauria*, 2nd ed. Berkeley: University of California Press, 2004.

## Chapter 2 – The Sauropods: Herbivorous Giants

Bakker, Robert T. "Ecology of the Brontosaurs." *Nature* 229 (January 15, 1971): 172–174.

———. *The Dinosaur Heresies*. New York, William Morrow: 1986.

Benton, Michael. *Vertebrate Paleontology*, 3rd ed. Oxford: Blackwell Publishing, 2005.

Bonnan, M.F. "Pes Anatomy in Sauropod Dinosaurs: Implications for Functional Morphology, Evolution, and Phylogeny." In *Thunder-Lizards: The Sauropodomorph Dinosaurs*, edited by K. Carpenter and V. Tidwell, Bloomington, Ind.: Indiana University Press. 2005. 346–380.

Bonnan, M.F. "The Evolution and Functional Morphology of Sauropod Dinosaur Locomotion." Ph.D. dissertation, Northern Illinois University (2001).

———. "The Evolution of Manus Shape in Sauropod Dinosaurs: Implications for Functional Morphology, Forelimb Orientation, and Phylogeny." *Journal of Vertebrate Paleontology* 23, no. 3 (September 2003): 595–613.

———. "Morphometric Analysis of Humerus and Femur Shape in Morrison Sauropods: Implications for Functional Morphology and Paleobiology." *Paleobiology* 30, no. 3, (2004): 444–470.

Bonnan, Matthew F., and Mathew J. Wedel. "First Occurrence of *Brachiosaurus* (Dinosauria: Sauropoda) from the Upper Jurassic Morrison Formation of Oklahoma." *PaleoBios* 24, no. 2 (September 15, 2004): 13–21.

Carpenter, Kenneth. *Eggs, Nests, and Baby Dinosaurs: A New Look at Dinosaur Reproduction*. Bloomington: Indiana University Press, 1999.

———, Karl F. Hirsch, John R. Horner, eds. *Dinosaur Eggs and Babies*. Cambridge: Cambridge University Press, 1994.

Chiappe, Luis M., Rodolfo A. Coria, Lowell Dingus, Frankie Jackson, Anusuya Chinsamy, and Marilyn Fox. "Sauropod Dinosaur Embryos from the Late Cretaceous of Patagonia." *Nature* 396 (November 19, 1998): 258–261.

Clarke, Tom. "Dinosaur Faces Rearranged." News@Nature.com. Available online. URL http://www.nature.com/news/2001/010809/full/news010809-2.html. Accessed December 11, 2007.

Colbert, Edwin H. *The Great Dinosaur Hunters and Their Discoveries.* New York: Dover Publications, 1984.

———. Raymond B. Cowles, and Charles M. Bogert. "Rates of Temperature Increase in the Dinosaurs." *Copeia* 1947, no. 2 (June 30, 1947): 141–142.

Currie, Philip J., and Kevin Padian, eds. *Encyclopedia of Dinosaurs.* New York: Academic Press, 1997.

Fastovsky, David E., and David B. Weishampel. *The Evolution and Extinction of the Dinosaurs,* 2nd ed. Cambridge: Cambridge University Press, 2005.

Gillooly, James F., Andrew P. Allen, and Eric L. Charnov. "Dinosaur Fossils Predict Body Temperatures." *PLoS Biology* 4, no. 8 (August 2006).

Hohnke, Lyle A., "Haemodynamics in the Sauropoda." *Nature* 244 (August 3, 1973): 309–310.

Hopkin, Michael. "Tiny Dino Discovered." News@Nature.com. Available online. URL http://www.nature.com/news/2006/060605/full/news060605-8.html. Accessed on December 11, 2007.

Kennedy, Elaine. "Dinosaur Gastroliths or 'Gastromyths'?" *Geoscience Reports,* No. 35 (Spring 2003): 1–4.

Ksepka, Daniel T., and Mark Norell. "*Erketu ellisoni,* a long-necked sauropod from Bor Guvé (Dornogov Aimag, Mongolia)." *American Museum Novitates* 3508 no. 1 (March 2006).

Lucas, Spencer G., Matthew C. Herne, Andrew B. Heckert, Adrian P. Hunt, and Robert M. Sullivan. "Reappraisal of *Seismosaurus,* a Late Jurassic Sauropod Dinosaur from New Mexico." *Proceedings,* Annual Meeting of the Society of Vertebrate Paleontology, November 7–10, 2004.

Norman, David. *Prehistoric Life: The Rise of the Vertebrates.* New York: Macmillan, 1994.

Pang, Qiqing, and Zhengwu Cheng. "A New Family of Sauropod Dinosaur from the Upper Cretaceous of Tianzhen, Shanxi Province, China." *Acta Geologica Sinica* 74, no. 2 (2000): 117–125.

Rauhut, Oliver W.M., Kristian Remes, Regina Fechner, Gerardo Cladera, and Pablo Puerta. "Discovery of a Short-Necked Sauropod Dinosaur from the Late Jurassic Period of Patagonia" *Nature* 435, no. 2 (June 2005): 670–672.

Rogers, Kristina Curry, and Catherine A. Forster. "The Last of the Dinosaur Titans: A New Sauropod from Madagascar." *Nature* 412 (August 2, 2001): 530–533.

Seymour, Roger S. "Dinosaurs, Endothermy and Blood Pressure." *Nature* 262 (July 15, 1976): 207–208.

Smith, Joshua B., Matthew C. Lamanna, Kenneth J. Lacovara, Peter Dodson, Jennifer R. Smith, Jason C. Poole, Robert Giegengack, and Yousry Attia. "A Giant Sauropod Dinosaur from an Upper Cretaceous Mangrove Deposit in Egypt. *Science* 292. no. 5522 (June 1, 2001): 1704–1706.

Stevens, K.A., and J.M. Parrish. "Neck Posture and Feeding Habits of Two Jurassic Sauropod Dinosaurs." *Science* 30, no. 284 (April 1999): 798–800.

———. "Neck Posture of Sauropod Dinosaurs." *Science* 30, no. 287 (January 28, 2000): 547b–547c.

Taylor, Michael P., and Darren Naish. "The Phylogenetic Taxonomy of Diplodocoidea (Dinosauria: Sauropoda)." *PaleoBios* 25, no. 2 (September 15, 2005): 1–7.

Upchurch, Paul. "Neck Posture of Sauropod Dinosaurs." *Science* 30, no. 287 (January 28, 2000): 547b.

———, and John Martin. "The Anatomy and Taxonomy of *Cetiosaurus* (Saurischia, Sauropoda) from the Middle Jurassic of England." *Journal of Vertebrate Paleontology* 23, no. 1 (March 2003): 208–231.

Wedel, Mathew J. "The Evolution of Vertebral Pneumaticity in Sauropod Dinosaurs." *Journal of Vertebrate Paleontology* 23, no. 2 (June 2003): 344–357.

———. "Vertebral Pneumaticity, Air Sacs, and the Physiology of Sauropod Dinosaurs." *Paleobiology*, Vol. 29, No. 2 (June 2003): 243–255.

———, Richard L. Cifelli, and R. Kent Sanders. "*Sauroposeidon Proteles,* a New Sauropod from the Early Cretaceous of Oklahoma." *Journal of Vertebrate Paleontology* 20, no. 1 (2000): 109–114.

Weishampel, David B., Peter Dodson, and Halszka Osmólska, eds. *The Dinosauria*, 2nd ed. Berkeley: University of California Press, 2004.

Wilson, Jeffrey A. "Sauropod Dinosaur Phylogeny: Critique and Cladistic Analysis." *Zoological Journal of the Linnean Society* 136, no. 2 (October 2002): 215.

———. "Redescription of the Mongolian Sauropod *Nemegtosaurus Mongoliensis* Nowinski (Dinosauria: Saurischia) and Comments on Late Cretaceous Sauropod Diversity." *Journal of Systematic Palaeontology* 3, no. 3 (August 24, 2005): 283–318.

## Chapter 3 – Theropod Diversity: Giant Predatory Dinosaurs

Abler, William L. "The Serrated Teeth of Tyrannosaurid Dinosaurs, and Biting Structure in Other Animals." *Paleobiology* 18, no. 2 (1992): 161–183.

———. "The Teeth of Tyrannosaurs." *Scientific American* (September 1999): 50–51.

Bakker, Robert T. *The Dinosaur Heresies*. New York, William Morrow, 1986.

———, and Peter M. Galton. "Dinosaur Monophyly and a New Class of Vertebrates." *Nature* 248 (March 8, 1974): 168–172.

Benton, Michael. *Vertebrate Paleontology*, 3rd ed. Oxford: Blackwell Publishing, 2005.

Buffetaut, Eric, Varavudh Suteethorn, and Haiyan Tong. "The Earliest Known Tyrannosaur from the Lower Cretaceous of Thailand." *Nature* 381 (June 20, 1996): 689–691.

Carpenter, Kenneth. "Variation in *Tyrannosaurus rex*." In *Dinosaur Systematics*, edited by Kenneth Carpenter and Philip J. Currie. Cambridge: Cambridge University Press, 1990.

Currie, Philip J., and Kevin Padian, eds. *Encyclopedia of Dinosaurs*. New York: Academic Press, 1997.

Farlow, James O., and M.K. Brett-Surman, eds. *The Complete Dinosaur*. Bloomington: Indiana University Press, 1999.

———, Stephen M. Gatesy, Thomas R. Holtz Jr., John R. Hutchinson, and John M. Robinson. "Theropod Locomotion." *American Zoologist* 40 (2000): 640–663.

———, Thomas R. Holtz Jr. "The Fossil Record of Predation in Dinosaurs." In *The Paleontological Society Papers* 8 (2002): 251–266.

Fastovsky, David E., and David B. Weishampel. *The Evolution and Extinction of the Dinosaurs*, 2nd ed. Cambridge: Cambridge University Press, 2005.

Franzosa, Jonathan William. "Evolution of the Brain in Theropoda (Dinosauria)." Ph.D. dissertation, The University of Texas at Austin (2004).

Gauthier, Jacques. "Feathered Dinosaurs, Flying Dinosaurs, Crown Dinosaurs, and the Name 'Aves.'" *New Perspectives on the Origin and Early Evolution of Birds.* New Haven: Peabody Museum of Natural History, Yale University (2001): 7–41.

Holtz, Thomas R. Jr. "A New Phylogeny of the Carnivorous Dinosaurs." *Gaia*, No. 15 (December 1998): 5–61.

Hutchinson, John R., and Mariano Garcia. "Tyrannosaurus Was Not a Fast Runner." *Nature* 415 (February 28, 2002): 1018–1022.

Lucas, Spencer G. *Dinosaurs: The Textbook*, 4th ed. New York: McGraw-Hill, 2004.

Norman, David. *Prehistoric Life: The Rise of the Vertebrates.* New York: Macmillan, 1994.

Rayfield, E.J. "Aspects of Comparative Cranial Mechanics." *Zoological Journal of the Linnean Society* 144, no. 3 (July 2005): 309.

———. "Cranial Design and Function in a Large Theropod Dinosaur." *Nature* 409 (February 22, 2001): 1033–1037.

Sanders, R.K., and D.K. Smith. "The Endocranium of the Theropod Dinosaur *Ceratosaurus* Studied with Computer Tomography." *Acta Palaeontologica Polonica* 50, no. 3 (2005): 601–616.

Stevens, Kent A. "Binocular Vision in Theropod Dinosaurs." *Journal of Vertebrate Paleontology* 26, no. 2 (June 2006): 321–330.

Weishampel, David B., Peter Dodson, and Halszka Osmólska, eds. *The Dinosauria*, 2nd ed. Berkeley: University of California Press, 2004.

Xu, Xing, James M. Clark, Catherine A. Forster, Mark Norell, Gregory M. Erickson, David A. Eberth, Chengkai Jia, and Qi Zhao. "A Basal Tyrannosauroid Dinosaur from the Late Jurassic of China." *Nature* 439 (2006): 715–718.

## Chapter 4 – Armored and Plated Dinosaurs: Ornithischian Innovations

Benton, Michael. *Vertebrate Paleontology*, 3rd ed. Oxford: Blackwell Publishing, 2005.

Carpenter, Kenneth, and Philip J. Currie, eds. *Dinosaur Systematics.* Cambridge: Cambridge University Press, 1990.

Colbert, Edwin H. *The Great Dinosaur Hunters and Their Discoveries.* New York: Dover Publications, 1984.

———, and Michael Morales. *Evolution of the Vertebrates*, 4th ed. New York: Wiley-LSS, 1991.

Currie, Philip J., and Kevin Padian, eds. *Encyclopedia of Dinosaurs*. New York: Academic Press, 1997.

Farlow, James O., and M.K. Brett-Surman, eds. *The Complete Dinosaur*. Bloomington: Indiana University Press, 1999.

Fastovsky, David E., and David B. Weishampel. *The Evolution and Extinction of the Dinosaurs*, 2nd ed. Cambridge: Cambridge University Press, 2005.

Lucas, Spencer G. *Dinosaurs: The Textbook*, 4th ed. New York: McGraw-Hill, 2004.

Norman, David. *Prehistoric Life: The Rise of the Vertebrates*. New York: Macmillan, 1994.

Paul, Gregory S. *Predatory Dinosaurs of the World*. New York: Simon and Schuster, 1988.

———, ed. *The Scientific American Book of Dinosaurs*. New York: St. Martin's Press, 2000.

Prothero, Donald R., and Robert H. Dott Jr. *Evolution of the Earth*. New York: McGraw-Hill, 2004.

Raven, Peter H., George B. Johnson, Jonathan B. Losos, and Susan R. Singer. *Biology,* 7th ed. New York: McGraw-Hill, 2005.

Romer, Alfred Sherwood. *Man and the Vertebrates*. Chicago: University of Chicago Press, 1933.

———, and Thomas S. Parsons. *The Vertebrate Body, Shorter Version*, 5th ed. Philadelphia: W.B. Saunders, 1978.

Ruben, John A., Terry D. Jones, and Nicholas R. Geist. "Respiratory and Reproductive Paleophysiology of Dinosaurs and Early Birds." *Physiological and Biochemical Zoology* 76 (2003): 141–164.

Schultz, Cesar Leandro, Claiton Marlon Dos Santos Scherer, and Mario Costa Barberena. "Biostratigraphy of Southern Brazilian Middle-Upper Triassic." *Revista Brasilerira de Geosciencias* 30, no. 3 (September 2000): 495–498.

Weishampel, David B., Peter Dodson, and Halszka Osmólska, eds. *The Dinosauria*, 2nd ed. Berkeley: University of California Press, 2004.

# FURTHER READING

Benton, Michael. *Vertebrate Paleontology*, 3rd ed. Oxford: Blackwell Publishing, 2005.

Carpenter, Kenneth. *Eggs, Nests, and Baby Dinosaurs: A New Look at Dinosaur Reproduction*. Bloomington: Indiana University Press, 1999.

———, and Philip J. Currie, eds. *Dinosaur Systematics*. Cambridge: Cambridge University Press, 1990.

———, Karl F. Hirsch, and John R. Horner, eds. *Dinosaur Eggs and Babies*. Cambridge: Cambridge University Press, 1994.

Charig, Alan. *A New Look at the Dinosaurs*. New York: Facts on File, 1983.

Colbert, Edwin H. *The Great Dinosaur Hunters and Their Discoveries*. New York: Dover Publications, 1984.

———, R.B. Cowles, and C.M. Bogert, "Temperature Tolerances in the American Alligator and Their Bearing on the Habits, Evolution, and Extinction of the Dinosaurs." *American Museum of Natural History Bulletin* 86 (1946): 327–374.

———, and Michael Morales. *Evolution of the Vertebrates*, 4th ed. New York: Wiley-LSS, 1991.

Currie, Philip J., and Kevin Padian, eds. *Encyclopedia of Dinosaurs*. New York: Academic Press, 1997.

Ellis, Richard. *No Turning Back: The Life and Death of Animal Species*. New York: Harper Collins, 2004.

Farlow, James O., and M.K. Brett-Surman, eds. *The Complete Dinosaur*. Bloomington: Indiana University Press, 1999.

Fastovsky, David E., and David B. Weishampel. *The Evolution and Extinction of the Dinosaurs*, 2nd ed. Cambridge: Cambridge University Press, 2005.

Fortey, Richard. *Life: A Natural History of the First Four Billion Years of Life on Earth*. New York: Alfred A. Knopf, 1998.

Gould, Stephen Jay, ed. *The Book of Life*. New York: W.W. Norton, 1993.

Jerison, H.J. *Evolution of the Brain and Intelligence.* New York: Academic Press, 1973: xiv, 482.

Lambert, David. *Encyclopedia of Prehistory.* New York: Facts on File, 2002.

Lucas, Spencer G. *Dinosaurs: The Textbook*, 4th ed. New York: McGraw-Hill, 2004.

Margulis, Lynn, and Karlene V. Schwartz. *Five Kingdoms: An Illustrated Guide to the Phyla of Life on Earth*, 3rd ed. New York: W.H. Freeman, 1998.

Norman, David. *Prehistoric Life: The Rise of the Vertebrates.* New York: Macmillan, 1994.

Palmer, Douglas. *Atlas of the Prehistoric World.* New York: Discovery Books, 1999.

Paul, Gregory S. *Predatory Dinosaurs of the World.* New York: Simon and Schuster, 1988.

———, ed. *The Scientific American Book of Dinosaurs.* New York: St. Martin's Press, 2000.

Prothero, Donald R., and Robert H. Dott Jr. *Evolution of the Earth.* New York: McGraw-Hill, 2004.

Raven, Peter H., George B. Johnson, Jonathan B. Losos, and Susan R. Singer. *Biology,* 7th ed. New York: McGraw-Hill, 2005.

Russell, Dale A. "Intelligence," *The Encyclopedia of Dinosaurs.* Edited by Philip J. Currie and Kevin Padian. San Diego: Academic Press, 1997: 371.

Weishampel, David B., Peter Dodson, and Halszka Osmólska, eds. *The Dinosauria*, 2nd ed. Berkeley: University of California Press, 2004.

Wilson, J.A., and Sereno, P.C. "Higher-level phylogeny of sauropod dinosaurs." *Journal of Vertebrate Paleontology*, Supplement 14:52A, 1994.

## Web Sites

### American Museum of Natural History. Vertebrate Evolution

An interactive diagram of vertebrate evolution with links to example fossil specimens in the world-famous collection of this museum.

**http://www.amnh.org/exhibitions/permanent/fossilhalls/vertebrate/**

## Bernard Price Institute For Palaeontological Research, University of the Witwatersrand, Johannesburg. Fossil Picture Gallery

Information is provided for a wide variety of South African vertebrate fossils by the Bernard Price Institute for Palaeontological Research.

http://www.wits.ac.za/geosciences/bpi/fossilpictures.htm

## Carnegie Museum of Natural History: Dinosaurs in Their Time

Online resource and view of the newly renovated dinosaur hall of one of America's leading natural history institutions.

http://www.carnegiemnh.org/dinosaurs/index.htm

## Chris Clowes's Paleontology Page

A privately compiled but exhaustive resource on many paleontology subjects, including a valuable look at the Burgess Shale fossils.

http://www.peripatus.gen.nz/Paleontology/Index.html

## International Commission on Stratigraphy. International Stratigraphic Chart

Downloadable geologic time scales provided by the International Commission on Stratigraphy.

http://www.stratigraphy.org/cheu.pdf

## Maddison, D.R., and K.-S. Schulz. The Tree of Life Web Project

The Tree of Life Web Project is a meticulously designed view of life-forms based on their phylogenetic (evolutionary) connections. It is hosted by the University of Arizona College of Agriculture and Life Sciences and the University of Arizona Library.

http://tolweb.org/tree/phylogeny.html

## Paleontology Portal. Vertebrates

A resource exploring early vertebrate life, produced by the University of California Museum of Paleontology, the Paleontological Society, the Society of Vertebrate Paleontology, and the United States Geological Survey.

http://www.paleoportal.org/index.php?globalnav=fossil_gallery&sectionnav=taxon&taxon_id=16

**Public Broadcasting Service. Evolution Library: Evidence for Evolution**

This resource outlines the extensive evidence in support of both the fact and theory of evolution, basing its approach on studies of the fossil record, molecular sequences, and comparative anatomy.

http://www.pbs.org/wgbh/evolution/library/04/

**Royal Tyrrell Museum of Palaeontology, Dinosaur Hall**

Virtual tour of the dinosaur fossil exhibit housing Canada's foremost collection of dinosaur fossils.

http://www.tyrrellmuseum.com/peek/index2.php?strSection=9

**Scotese, Christopher R. Paleomap Project**

A valuable source of continental maps showing the positioning of Earth's continents over the course of geologic time.

http://www.scotese.com/

**Virtual Fossil Museum. Fossils Across Geological Time and Evolution**

A privately funded, image-rich educational resource dedicated to fossils. Contributors include amateur and professional paleontologists.

http://www.fossilmuseum.net/index.htm

# PICTURE CREDITS

# INDEX

# ABOUT THE AUTHOR

**THOM HOLMES** is a writer specializing in natural history subjects and dinosaurs. He is noted for his expertise on the early history of dinosaur science in America. He was the publications director of *The Dinosaur Society* for six years (1991–1997) and the editor of its newsletter, *Dino Times*, the world's only monthly publication devoted to news about dinosaur discoveries. It was through the Society and his work with the Academy of Natural Sciences in Philadelphia that Thom developed widespread contacts and working relationships with paleontologists and paleo-artists throughout the world.

Thom's published works include *Fossil Feud: The Rivalry of America's First Dinosaur Hunters* (Silver Burdett Press, September 1997); *The Dinosaur Library* (Enslow, 2001–2002); *Duel of the Dinosaur Hunters* (Pearson Education, 2002); *Fossil Feud: The First American Dinosaur Hunters* (Silver Burdett/Julian Messner, 1997). His many honors and awards include the National Science Teachers Association's *Outstanding Science Book of 1998*, VOYA's 1997 Nonfiction Honor List, an Orbis Pictus Honor, and the Chicago Public Library Association's *"Best of the Best"* in science books for young people.

Thom did undergraduate work in geology and studied paleontology through his role as a staff educator with the Academy of Natural Sciences in Philadelphia. He is a regular participant in field exploration, with two recent expeditions to Patagonia in association with Canadian, American, and Argentinian universities.